CLAIRE TOMALIN

SHELLEY

AND HIS WORLD

with 104 illustrations

THAMES AND HUDSON

for Michael

Half-title: Lerici in *c.* 1826 by
Bonington. 'The scene was . . . of
unimaginable beauty. The blue
extent of waters, the almost
landlocked bay, the near castle of
Lerici shutting it in to the left . . .'
(Mary Shelley)

Facing title-page: detail from Amelia
Curran's 1819 portrait of Shelley,
completed after his death and not
thought a good likeness by those
who knew him

OUTSIDE THE VILLAGE OF WARNHAM in Sussex is a pond as big as a small lake, surrounded by meadows set with tall and splendid trees, a paradisal place for a boy to spend a summer's day. The earliest letter of Shelley's that we know – he was eleven when he wrote it – was addressed to his cousin Kate, inviting her and her brother Tom to spend a day, with a picnic, at the pond, where his father kept a pleasure boat. To the end of his life, boats and water, trees and grass were his symbols of blessedness, Arcadia and Elysium in one. They dwelt in his imagination, in his poetry, in the drawings scattered about his notebooks. Yet Shelley was not a pastoral writer. What interested him was the power of free thought and the spirit of revolution; and these led him to break away from the privileged security that seemed to be his birthright.

Percy Bysshe Shelley was born in 1792, a year of portents. The English could hardly take their eyes from France, where the momentum of revolution had carried the king to prison and stripped the aristocracy and the church of their power and possessions; even domestic tyranny was under attack, with the first divorce laws passed. For some in England all this was inspiration. Tom Paine travelled the country, enthusiastically greeted by local revolutionary societies, and in London political clubs called for parliamentary reform and universal male suffrage. Paine published the second part of his *Rights of Man*,

One of many sketches of boats, trees and water from Shelley's notebooks

The statue of Louis XIV toppled by the crowd, Paris, Place des Victoires, 1792

and an ex-governess, Mary Wollstonecraft, published her *Vindication of the Rights of Woman*, both books that were to influence Shelley profoundly. A third was on the point of completion: William Godwin's master-work, *Enquiry Concerning Political Justice*. In Germany a young Englishman, James Lawrence, was working on a book proposing the abolition of marriage and total sexual and economic emancipation of women; this too would make its mark on Shelley. And a trio who were to give him his belief in the power of poetry to enter and change men's minds were just reaching maturity: Wordsworth at twenty-two visiting France, full of revolutionary enthusiasm; Coleridge and Southey both university radicals.

But, for the majority of the English, any initial sympathy with the French Revolution was draining away in 1792 as reports of disorder and bloodshed grew worse. William Cowper withdrew his cautious approval, and Blake, who had been seen wearing a scarlet Jacobin cap, is said to have put it off. 'O! that France had possessed the wisdom of knowing where to stop!' lamented the poet Anna Seward to her colleague Helen Maria Williams, resident in Paris. The novelist Fanny Burney, always nervous of the Revolution, took comfort from a talk with Edmund Burke over a Hampstead dinner table; he told her that even Charles James Fox had 'too much taste for such a Revolution'. When Burke was ribbed gently by his brother for his reactionary views, he turned to Miss Burney, filled her wineglass and

drank a toast, 'Come, then – here's *Slavery forever!*' This was the year in which Burke split the Whig party, taking the majority over to support the Tories who wanted war with France. And war came in February 1793, bringing great misery to England, draining its finances and speeding inflation. The poor, both in the country and in the new industrial towns of the north, were brought to near-starvation. War meant too a vast build-up of armed forces, so that England began to look like an occupied country, with barracks everywhere and a discontented militia set over a powerless and embittered people. Finally, it meant that the upper and educated classes, accustomed to travel in Europe and enjoy its arts and ideas, were to be virtually confined to their own small island for two decades; it was at the end of this period that the word 'insular' began to be used in the sense of narrow-minded and prejudiced.

At Field Place in Sussex the world had already shrunk. True, the forty-year-old squire, Timothy Shelley, had been in parliament as a Whig protégé of the reforming Duke of Norfolk; but he was now unseated and had also recently found himself a wife, Elizabeth Pilfold, a handsome and well-bred young woman of twenty-nine. On 4 August their first child was born, in a room that looked out over the green garden to the fields and woods beyond. He was a blue-eyed boy and he was christened Percy Bysshe, and known thereafter in the family by his second name.

Field Place, near Horsham, as it was in 1792

7

Castle Goring, grandiose but unfinished project of the poet's grandfather, Sir Bysshe

Sir Bysshe Shelley. 'He is a bad man. I never had respect for him: I always regarded him as a curse on society.' (Shelley in 1812)

The Shelleys were an established Sussex family, but this particular branch had come into its prosperity only recently. Bysshe's grandfather, also Bysshe, was born in very modest circumstances in New Jersey, in America, and had to come to England to acquire a large fortune, chiefly by means of eloping with two successive heiresses. Old Bysshe educated his eldest son Timothy by sending him to Oxford and on the Grand Tour. He also built an enormous mansion, Castle Goring, for his family; but nobody wanted to live in it. Even he preferred to spend days in a cottage and evenings at the inn, when he was not visiting his mistress Mrs Nicholls and their four children – one actually called Bysshe – in Lambeth. Eccentric in some respects, he was a traditionalist in others: he was set on leaving a large, secure capital of money and estates for his legitimate male descendants, sharing fully in the belief of his day that the supreme value of the family resided in the prosperity of the male heirs. The granting of a baronetcy in 1806 put society's official seal of approval on the Shelleys.

Bysshe was followed by five little sisters, one dying in infancy. For his first decade he lived at home, dominating this small female court; the pleasures of the situation may account for his lifelong propensity for setting up households of women around himself. His third sister Hellen remembered him as always good-tempered, full of pranks and vividly imaginative. He and his closest sister, Elizabeth, were supposed to resemble one another as though they had been twins, and from very early days they wrote verses together. He had a pony to gallop on and was taught field sports; shooting he loved all his life, although he came to prefer inanimate targets. At six he went daily to the local clergyman's house for Latin lessons. His memory was remarkable and his sisters remembered him reciting Latin verses to their father, who was proud of his accomplished son. It was a kind, conventional family. And when Bysshe was ten he was sent, conventionally, away to school.

A Cat in distress
Nothing more or less
Good folks I must faithfully tell ye
As I am a sinner
It wants for some dinner
To stuff out its own little belly

2

You mightn't easily guess
All the modes of distress
Which torture the tenants of earth
And the various evils
Which like many devils
Attend the poor dogs from their birth

3

Some a living require
And others desire
An old fellow out of the way

Shelley (*right*) was about ten when the Duc de Montpensier is believed to have drawn him on a visit to Penshurst. At the same age he wrote *A Cat in Distress*, his first known poem, here fair-copied and illustrated by his sister Elizabeth (*above right*)

The Syon House Academy at Brentford was run by a gruff Dr Greenlaw and his wife; there were about sixty boys rising to the age of eighteen and as rough as any such group of boys is likely to be. Shelley's older cousin Tom Medwin, who was already there, says the place was 'a perfect hell' to the slight, girlish-looking child. He took refuge in solitary musing and the reading of Gothic romances, the cheapest and most plentiful popular entertainment in print then; they sated his appetite for reading and excited his imagination with ghosts and terrors.

The school did offer Shelley one thing that caught his interest. A travelling lecturer, Dr Adam Walker, friend of the great radical scientist Joseph Priestley, came to speak to the boys about chemistry and the scientific advances of the day. Impressed by the talk of electricity, telescopes and magnetism, Shelley carried home his enthusiasm to share with his admiring and sometimes frightened sisters. There was a plan to cure their chilblains by passing electric currents through them; on another occasion, putting science to the service of fiction, he persuaded them to dress up as fiends and accompany him as he pranced through the house with a bowl of burning spirits in his hand; and he mysteriously hinted of an alchemist living concealed in a certain room in the attic.

Luigi Galvani's experiments of the 1780s drew attention to the relation of animal function to electricity, a subject that fascinated Shelley throughout his life

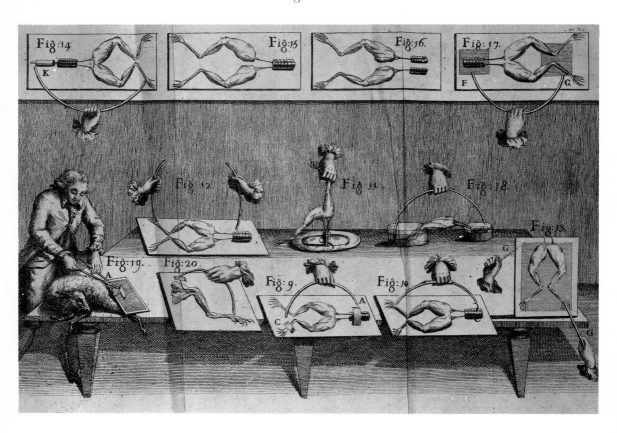

Eton: the idyllic view

His two years' initiation into the rougher world of boys was a preparation for Eton. There he remained for six years, the longest stable residence of his life, from 1804 to 1810. (While he was there the youngest Shelley child, John, was born in 1806.) Dr Keate, known as 'Flogger', became Provost during Shelley's time, but the masters were less troublesome to him than the boys, who at once perceived that they had someone odd to bait and took great pleasure in driving gentle Shelley into a mad, white, shaking and raging creature. In later years his friend Thomas Love Peacock and his wife Mary were to hear of his intense sufferings and also of how he once stabbed another boy with a fork in his anger.

There was much for Shelley to find objectionable at Eton:

> there rose
> From the near schoolroom, voices, that, alas!
> Were but one echo from a world of woes –
> The harsh and grating strife of tyrants and of foes.

– is how he put it later; and 'nothing that my tyrants knew or taught / I cared to learn'. He detested the fagging system, whereby younger boys bought protection from older ones by performing menial services for them: '*obedience* is a word which in my opinion should have no existence', he told his father later. Studies were virtually confined to the reading of Latin and Greek and making of verses in those languages, child's play to Shelley but not calculated to hold his attention; he was much more interested in chemistry. Lacking instruction, he was drawn by the quasi-magical power of science, and had not the temperament for slow, patiently repeated experiment and

William Godwin (1756–1836),
hailed by Shelley as 'the
regulator and former of my mind'

observation. In visionary fashion, he imagined a world transformed by electricity, Africa explored by balloon, infertile soil made productive. Pursuing such prophetic notions, he forgot to tie his shoelaces or wear a hat; to his conventional peers such opinions and behaviour earned him the title of 'mad Shelley'.

The intellectual guidance and companionship he failed to find at Eton were provided in his last two years there by the elderly Dr James Lind, one of George III's physicians, who lived in Windsor and took a fancy to the clever, enthusiastic boy. Lind, Edinburgh-born and connected with the radical, scientific Lunar Society that flourished in the 1780s and brought together men such as Joseph Priestley, Erasmus Darwin and James Watt, had also travelled as far afield as India and China. He was a prime instance of British Enlightenment man and he played a crucial part in Shelley's development.

Under Lind's influence Shelley began to learn modern languages – French and German – and to read seriously. He absorbed the works of Lucretius (*De rerum natura*), whose anti-religious views pleased him, Pliny (*Historia naturalis*), Franklin and Condorcet, another deeply anti-religious writer whose views on human progress and perfectibility made a permanent mark on his thinking. He also discovered the English philosopher who was to shape the course of his life dramatically: William Godwin. No doubt Shelley was drawn first to Godwin's novel *St Leon*, whose hero possesses the Elixir Vitae and the Philosopher's Stone. But he went on to read *Political Justice* and make its serenely reasonable and optimistic principles his own. *Political Justice* is in essence an attack on government – which Godwin described as intending to suppress injustice but actually embodying and perpetuating it – and indeed on all institutions which ossify behaviour and thinking. By free inquiry, Godwin believed that mankind would necessarily arrive at a state of contented anarchy; crime and even insincerity would slowly disappear, and the equal distribution of wealth would be accepted by all as an essential basis for human happiness. To Shelley, as to the young Wordsworth, these ideas came with the force of revelation.

Eton undoubtedly caused him to suffer, and he was at times inclined to describe it as a microcosm of the evils of the world at large. But his memories were not all black. He made some friends with whom he enjoyed exploring the gentle Berkshire fields and woods along the banks of the Thames, and the lines he wrote in 1821 in *The Boat on the Serchio* suggest good moments:

> Those bottles of warm tea –
> (Give me some straw) – must be stowed tenderly;
> Such as we used, in summer after six,
> To cram in greatcoat pockets, and to mix
> Hard eggs and radishes and rolls at Eton,
> And, couched on stolen hay in those green harbours
> Farmers call gaps, and we schoolboys called arbours,
> Would feast till eight.

In his last school year he published a novel, *Zastrozzi*, giving a

banquet for eight of his friends with part of the proceeds; this is not the action of a wholly isolated and martyred boy.

Zastrozzi is a Gothic tale of vengeance and passion, closely modelled on the trash Shelley had comforted himself with at Syon Academy. The plot turns on the pursuit of a dazed hero by a wicked beauty determined to seduce him, and concludes with general bloodshed. Shelley put his initials on the title-page, and an epigraph taken from *Paradise Lost*, the earliest token of his lifelong admiration for Milton, whose career as both political pamphleteer and poet he would emulate.

He was already writing poetry. Just after leaving school, and due to go to Oxford in October 1810, he published his first volume, *Original Poetry by Victor and Cazire*. It contained some rattling verse epistles by his sister Elizabeth and sentimental lyrics, Gothic ballads and alleged translations from the German and Italian by Bysshe. If booby prizes were given for the juvenilia of great poets, *Victor and Cazire* would carry one off. To crown matters, it included an entire poem lifted from the Gothic author known as 'Monk' Lewis; when the publisher asked Shelley about this he offered no explanation, but insisted on the

'Sometimes between the wide and flowering meadows, Mile after mile we sailed, and 'twas delight To see far off the sunbeams chase the shadows Over the grass . . .' (*Revolt of Islam*)

This portrait, attributed to
Lawrence and supposed to be of
Shelley in about 1810, has been
the property of a Devon family
for over 100 years, but its
provenance is unknown

destruction of all unsold copies. Nearly 1,500 had been printed; the
episode leaves a small question-mark over his reliability and judg-
ment, boy as he was.

A copy of *Victor and Cazire* was sent by Shelley to his cousin Harriet
Grove in Wiltshire. It was not an idle gift. Harriet's mother and Mrs
Shelley were sisters, the families very close and a mutual attraction
between the cousins smiled upon. The girl, a year older than Bysshe,
was pretty and affectionate; her diary could have been penned by one
of Jane Austen's young ladies. She records a great many walks, games
of battledore, bathing in the sea and dances. She reads a little: Sterne's
Sentimental Journey and an anti-Godwinite novel, *The Modern Philosophers*.
It made her laugh, but would have outraged Shelley, who fell in love
with her and wished to convert her to his views.

Her devotion to her Etonian cousin, 'dear Bysshe' and then 'dearest Percy', is evident. The high point is reached when both families stay in London in the spring of 1810 and the young pair are allowed a good deal of licence, walking in Lincoln's Inn Fields and disliking the opera together. But by the end of the year she has nothing more to say of him, and by January 1811 Shelley is agonizedly attributing their severance to her disapproval of his anti-religious views. Possibly this was so; there is no sign of family pressure in her diary and attempts to eradicate references to him suggest that she suffered her own change of heart. She married a neighbouring landowner's son and lived the sort of uneventful life poets wish on their daughters more often than their mistresses. For Shelley, the year 1811 was to see him carried irrevocably out of the world of custom and ceremony.

Oxford in 1810 was more of a finishing school for well-to-do young men than a place of learning, run by college Fellows who were obliged to take Holy Orders. According to Jeremy Bentham most were morose, insipid or profligate. The Bodleian, one of the finest libraries in Europe, went almost unused. University College, where Shelley was to go, differed in no way from the rest; even the young niece of the Master, paying a visit from Scotland, delivered the tart verdict that 'the very meaning of the word education did not seem to be understood'.

Lincoln's Inn Fields. 'Walked in the Fields with dear Bysshe then went shopping & had great fun left Aunt & Mama. . . . Aunt S — says she shall send for a Chain & Chain us to her —' (Harriet Grove's diary, 26 April 1810)

Oxford in its rural setting

Still, Shelley arrived with every prospect of being comfortable. He was attending his father's college; Timothy, proudly escorting him, had his rooms newly furnished. He also took his son to see the Oxford booksellers and printers, Slatter & Munday, to whom he made the most famous remark of his life: 'My son here has a literary turn; he is already an author, and do pray indulge him in his printing freaks.'

A few days later another important meeting took place when, over dinner in hall, Shelley came face to face with Thomas Jefferson Hogg, son of a Yorkshire barrister and a vigorous and original young man. An immediate and passionate friendship sprang up between the two. Hogg's portrait of Shelley, written from the vantage point of somewhat cynical middle age, still breathes a strong, sardonic affection, and the Oxford chapters are particularly engaging.

Through his eyes we see Shelley, tall, slight and stooped, going about Oxford with his characteristic hasty step, coatless and open-necked; hear his high, cracked voice; see him reading with the book always held right up to his eyes, or lying so close to the fire that he seemed more salamander than mortal. Now he is running headlong into his sported oak – the outer door to college rooms – and now tramping through the Oxfordshire mud with his pistols, enraged when a farm dog tears the skirts of his new, blue, brass-buttoned tailcoat, delighted with a paper boat or a conversation with a gypsy child. His view of the dons was lordly:

'They are very dull people here,' Shelley said to me one evening . . . 'a little man sent for me this morning, and told me in an almost inaudible whisper that I must read: "you must read", he said many times in his small voice. . . . I told him I had some books in my pocket, and began to take them out. He stared at me, and said that was not exactly what he meant: "you must read *Prometheus Vinctus*, and Demosthenes *de Coronâ*, and Euclid." "Must I read Euclid?" I asked sorrowfully. . . .'

Hogg's description of Shelley's rooms transforms them into a sorcerer's cave:

Books, boots, papers, shoes, philosophical instruments, clothes, pistols, linen, crockery, ammunition, and phials innumerable, with money, stockings, prints, crucibles, bags, and boxes were scattered on the floor and in every place. . . . The tables, and especially the carpet, were already stained with large spots of various hues, which frequently proclaimed the agency of fire. An electrical machine, an air pump, the galvanic trough, a solar microscope, and large glass jars and receivers, were conspicuous amidst the mass of matter.

By the end of his first term Shelley had decided that Hogg must bind their friendship still closer by wooing his sister Elizabeth. Letters from Field Place elaborated on this plan alongside laments over the 'uncongenial jollities of Xmas', the loss of Harriet and some fierce disputes with his father over the question of religious faith. Mrs Shelley became alarmed by her son's tendencies too: 'My mother fancies me on the High Road to Pandemonium, she fancies I want to make a deistical coterie of all my little sisters.' And it was true that Shelley was now able to assail conventional Christian belief with every logical weapon from the Enlightenment armoury.

Thomas Jefferson Hogg (1792–1862) as an undergraduate

His father's hope was that he would enter for a poetry prize when he returned for the Lent term. He had published a second novel, *St Irvyne, or the Rosicrucian*, 'by a Gentleman of the University of Oxford', written to much the same formula as *Zastrozzi* but with additional supernatural elements. Although it was now on display in Slatter & Munday's window it deserved to be, and was, a failure. Another publication was a volume of poems, *Posthumous Fragments of Margaret Nicholson* by 'John Fitzvictor'. The humour of the title was that Mrs Nicholson was a mad washerwoman who had attempted to kill George III in 1786; it was not much of a joke, and the poems are inept whether political, erotic or lamenting lost happiness. But here and there a glimpse of later themes appears. An invocation to despair contains a Shelleyan turn of phrase:

> Arise ye sightless spirits of the storm,
> Ye unseen minstrels of the aërial song . . .

and another poem produces a characteristic encounter: 'I met a maniac, like he was to me.' This was not a merely poetic notion; Shelley told Hogg and other friends that 'I myself am often mad'. His cousin Medwin believed that 'insanity hung as by a hair suspended over the head of Shelley' and there were times when not only his family but also, later, so close and sympathetic an observer as Thomas Love Peacock took the view that his behaviour passed beyond the bounds of the normal.

Leigh Hunt (1784–1859), radical editor and poet, who became Shelley's lifelong friend – and dependant

In March Shelley wrote to his father saying he was getting on with his prize poem on the Parthenon. He was also quietly busy with other interests. He subscribed a guinea to a fund for an Irish journalist, Peter Finnerty, sentenced to prison for political outspokenness, and offered to write a poem in his defence; and wrote to Leigh Hunt, editor of the liberal magazine, the *Examiner*, who had tangled with the powers of the land more than once. To Hunt, Shelley suggested that he intended to follow his father into parliament.

Meanwhile, he had printed a very short pamphlet claiming the necessity for free inquiry into religious belief and suggesting that the existence of God remained unproven by physical evidence, reason or testimony. He called it *The Necessity of Atheism*, the title markedly more pugnacious than the contents; and when the copies arrived he sent some off to various bishops and heads of colleges. He also went into Slatter & Munday's shop and laid some out on the counters, where they remained for twenty minutes until they caught the eye of a passing Fellow of New College, who went into the shop and easily persuaded the astonished proprietors to burn them all at once. Shelley now sent a copy to the Professor of Poetry, accompanied by a letter signed 'Jeremiah Stukely'. The Professor showed this to the Master of University College, who in turn summoned Shelley on the morning of 25 March. In the presence of a few irritated Fellows, first Shelley and then Hogg refused to answer questions as to the authorship of the pamphlet and both were summarily expelled from the University. According to Hogg, Shelley was in a state of acute excitement and distress.

The two young men arrived in London the next day, found themselves a room in a coffee house and called at once on Harriet Grove's brothers in Lincoln's Inn Fields where, according to Hogg, they were rather quietly received at first. Shelley was desperate to talk. At four in the morning he roused another cousin, Tom Medwin, knocking and laughing and calling out 'I am expelled – for atheism'. The next morning he and Hogg set out to find proper lodgings, alighting in rooms off Oxford Street which caught Shelley's fancy because they were papered in a pattern of green and purple grapes on a trellis. Here they settled, planning to resume their reading and walking habits and to stay together. The Grove cousins proved friendly; John was a surgeon, Charles a medical student, and Shelley attended a course of lectures on anatomy at St Bartholomew's Hospital with a fleeting thought of taking up medicine himself. He also went with them to a debating club, where he attracted attention as a speaker but fled without giving his name.

Two of his sisters, Hellen and Mary, were at boarding school on Clapham Common, where Shelley had already met their friend Harriet Westbrook, who was quite prepared to join them in sympathetic hero-worship of Bysshe. Harriet was fifteen, the prettiest girl in the school, with brilliant pink cheeks, a vast quantity of curls and a perfect readiness to listen to Shelley's opinions and adopt them as her own. Not surprisingly, he found some comfort in his visits to Clapham.

Timothy Shelley's reaction to the news of his son's expulsion was to come to London, attempt to separate him from Hogg, whom he at first blamed, and insist that Shelley should return home and take instruction from a clergyman. When the two met, the father cursed, wept and insisted on reading out Archbishop Paley's arguments for the existence of God. The son laughed derisively, the more so because his father mispronounced Paley as 'Pally'. Both were slightly hysterical. A little later, Mrs Shelley privately sent her son money for his journey home; but he returned it.

Money now became of prime importance in the struggle, and Timothy Shelley continued to use it as his weapon until his death. Old Sir Bysshe supported Timothy against young Bysshe, and it was decided that he must cool his heels and deal only through the family lawyer, Whitton. Shelley stood to inherit over £200,000 in due course; he showed his disregard for the values of his family by suggesting to Whitton that the entail, which covered £80,000 of the estate, should be set aside and that part divided between Mrs Shelley and the girls. He would be content, meanwhile, with an annuity of £100 or £200 a year. Timothy was almost as much shocked by this piece of disrespect for property as by his son's atheism. And although Shelley came to hate the poverty in which he lived most of his life, and was sometimes culpably careless about debts, he was never acquisitive and never wanted anything more than a competence for himself.

Clapham Common, where Shelley's sisters went to school and their friend Harriet Westbrook was threatened with 'persecution' for adopting Shelley's views

Details from Romney's portraits
of Sir Timothy and Lady Shelley

In mid-April Hogg, won over and forgiven by his family, departed for a holiday before going home to York to take up legal studies. Deprived of his friend, Shelley was naturally lonely. He kept a journal in which he described his dreams, and began to sleepwalk as he had done in times of stress at school and would again when life was difficult. Sometimes Medwin went to Kensington Gardens with him and watched him sail boats on the Serpentine; there were still the Grove brothers; and now the Westbrooks – for Harriet had a much older sister, Eliza – began to fill up the emptiness. Harriet is reported as reading Voltaire in May, and being persecuted at school for the atheism she has learnt from Shelley. Her father, a well-to-do coffee house proprietor, no doubt saw the advantage of his daughter's friendship with the rich, susceptible heir to a baronetcy and fortune, and Shelley was made welcome at the Westbrook house. By the time he left London for Sussex in May, he had arranged that Harriet and he should correspond; but her letters were to go to his uncle Pilfold's house at Cuckfield, not to Field Place.

Shelley went to Cuckfield because this maternal uncle was friendly and prepared to help the warring father and son to an agreement of sorts. Bysshe was to have £200 a year and live where he chose; he also agreed to take up a profession. His mother, he told Hogg, with whom he corresponded unceasingly, was 'quite rational'. 'She says . . . if a man is a good man, atheist or Xtian he will do very well in whatever future state awaits us. This I call liberality.' But his sister Elizabeth was decidedly cool, especially when he attempted to press Hogg's love on her – a love dreamed up out of the air by Shelley, for the two had not met. Shelley's letters were full of attacks on the institution of marriage, and his hope was that Hogg and his sister would form a free love union. A clandestine visit by Hogg in which he was smuggled into Field Place and kept concealed in Shelley's room did nothing to further the suit.

Shelley was cheered through the confusions of these months by a new friend, Elizabeth Hitchener, a Sussex schoolmistress who taught one of his Pilfold cousins. Miss Hitchener was ten years older than Shelley and the daughter of an innkeeper; she was unusual in her abilities and independence of mind (and also in physical appearance, for she was strikingly tall and dark). She inclined to feminism and republicanism: opinions of this kind had to be kept to oneself in Sussex in 1811. The friendship and correspondence with Shelley must have been a huge relief from intellectual isolation. He in turn wrote to her that, although he was cautious in his theological speculations,

in politics – here I am enthusiastic. I have reasoned, and my reason has brought me on this subject to the end of my inquiries. I am no aristocrat, nor 'crat' at all, but vehemently long for the time when men may dare to live in accordance with Nature and Reason – in consequence, with Virtue, to which I firmly believe that Religion and its establishments, Polity and its establishments, are the formidable though destructible barriers.

And he complained, very reasonably, of the folly of the Prince Regent's ball at Carlton House in June, for which £120,000 was spent on splendours that included an artificial stream in which goldfish swam between moss banks – all this when bad harvests and inflation had brought the people to terrible distress, the Lancashire mill workers were on a three-day week and machines were being smashed. Shelley began an English version of the *Marseillaise* with the lines

Tremble, kings despised of man!
Ye traitors to your Country . . .

Poor George III, grief-struck at the death of his youngest daughter, had, in fact, lapsed into madness again. All through 1811 signs of his recovery were looked for in vain while his son prepared to take over the position of ruling monarch by abandoning any liberal principles he had once boasted.

Shelley's political views had now taken permanent shape. He had absorbed the lessons of Condorcet, Thomas Paine and Godwin, all of whom believed in the power of the human mind to change the circumstances of life for the better unless prevented by established institutions such as the monarchy and the church; but all of whom equally developed reservations about overthrowing them by violence. He had also observed for himself the gulf between rich and poor, usually justified to young people of his class by reference to the will of God. To Shelley, this explanation was unacceptable. For the rest of his life he remained true to his detestation of monarchy, aristocracy, huge fortunes, the established church and standing armies. He remained a reformer, always hoping to see reform brought about by reasonable means and despairing when blood was shed even by insurgents with a just cause; and he retained his belief in the necessity of redistributing wealth.

He also retained his dislike of the institution of marriage as a tie unnecessary between those who care for one another and terrible between those who do not. In spite of this he was persuaded to marry in 1811, partly because he saw the force of the argument that free love, in the social and medical circumstances of the day, was likely to put women into more difficulties than men. He was also captivated by Harriet Westbrook's beauty, distress and trust in him; and perhaps made more vulnerable by the estrangement from a family of sisters and girl cousins who had been supremely important to him all through his early years. Defiance of his father was another good reason for marrying: Timothy Shelley (according to Medwin) told him that he would provide for any number of bastards but would not forgive a *mésalliance*. Such a remark from an uncongenial father to an idealistic boy of eighteen is calculated to put him on the path of knight errantry; and Shelley, like his friend Leigh Hunt, was shocked by the sexual callousness of a society which used armies of prostitutes while professing to observe Christian ideals of marriage.

After spending a week in London in early July, and seeing the Westbrooks again, Shelley paid a visit to his cousin Thomas Grove's estate, Cwm Elan, in Wales. From there he wrote to both Hogg and Miss Hitchener to say that Harriet was in love with him, had told him so, was suffering persecution at school and had thrown herself on his protection. She meanwhile sent him a copy of a book by Amelia Opie, onetime friend of William Godwin and his wife Mary Wollstonecraft; the point of Mrs Opie's novel, *Adeline Mowbray*, was to show the evils arising from even a principled decision not to marry, the heroine's position becoming really desperate when she finds herself pregnant. Possibly Shelley knew by now that his hero Godwin had himself succumbed to a marriage ceremony with Mary Wollstonecraft in just those circumstances.

At all events, on 25 August Shelley and Harriet – who were now just nineteen and sixteen respectively – met in London, spent the day hiding in a coffee house, and took the night coach for Scotland where they were married, after three days of almost non-stop travel. He had less than £50 of borrowed money in his pockets. Within a few days of the wedding he persuaded Hogg to join him and Harriet in Edinburgh, setting up the pattern of a *ménage* of at least three which he found essential to happiness. Hogg was enchanted by Harriet, and the three of them spent their time reading and translating – Shelley began on the French naturalist and historian Buffon, Harriet on a French romance – and visiting the Edinburgh kirks to laugh at the sermons. In the evenings Harriet read aloud while, according to Hogg, her husband fell asleep on the hearth-rug.

The chief problem was money. As soon as Timothy heard of his son's marriage he stopped his allowance. Shelley wrote angry complaints to both his father and his grandfather:

> The institutions of society have made you, tho' liable to be misled by passion and prejudice like others, the *Head of the family* . . .

– a situation Shelley himself could not be imagined in; and later,

> Think not I am an insect whom injuries destroy – had I money enough I would meet you in London, & hollow in your ears Bysshe, Bysshe, Bysshe, – aye Bysshe till you're deaf.

He went so far as to accuse his father of wishing him dead, developing a fantasy that he would have liked him conscripted for the Peninsular War and killed in Spain. He also made a wild accusation of adultery against his mother, fortunately not seen by the family, since by then all letters were passed unopened to Whitton.

Early in October the three runaways left Edinburgh for York, so that Hogg could continue his studies. Shelley now informed Miss Hitchener, after several weeks' silence, that he was married, and her warm response led him to hail her as sister of his soul; in addition, he proposed that she should come and live as part of his household. Eliza Westbrook was also summoned. Meanwhile, he set off for Sussex again, leaving Harriet and Hogg in York. His trip was a vain one; he got no money and was further estranged from his mother and sisters; Whitton referred to him as 'a mad viper'. He returned to York in low spirits to find a crisis there too. In his absence, Harriet told him, Hogg had attempted to seduce her; and she and Eliza Westbrook insisted on leaving York at once, without informing Hogg. Shelley was in agony; his love for Hogg was as great as his love for Harriet and, as he wrote to Elizabeth Hitchener, 'his vices and not himself were the objects of my horror'. Impassioned letters of mingled reproach, forgiveness and desolation at losing his friend flew from Keswick, where the Shelley party had fled, to York. He attempted to explain that it was not his prejudice that stood between the friends:

> Jealousy has no place in my bosom, I am indeed at times very much inclined to think that the Godwinian plan is best. . . . But Harriet does not think so. She is prejudiced; tho I hope she will not always be so – And on her opinions of right and wrong alone does the morality of the present case depend.

Possibly he would have shared Harriet gladly with Hogg had she been willing; but she was not, and his spirits were in turmoil, whether from simple disappointment at Hogg's baseness or a more complicated response to the effect of marriage on friendship.

By the end of November he was calmer. He and Harriet and Eliza were settled at Chestnut Cottage, one of a group a mile outside Keswick. He began to notice the scenery and describe it:

> These gigantic mountains piled on each other, these water-falls, these million-shaped clouds tinted by the varying colours of innumerable rainbows hanging between yourself and the lake as smooth and dark as a plain of polished jet . . .

On 1 December the party went to stay at Greystoke, the house of the Duke of Norfolk, who was trying to reconcile the father and son. Shelley did agree to write a letter of apology, though insisting that he would not conceal his political or religious opinions, and Timothy relented: the allowance was restored.

Charles Howard, 11th Duke of Norfolk (1746–1815), a convivial radical. 'He desires and votes for Reform, tho' he has not virtue enough to begin it in his own person' commented Shelley severely

Shelley's love of the Lakeland poets' work drew him to the Lakes and he shared their enthusiasm for the scenery, portrayed here by Turner

One of his hopes in going to the Lakes was to meet Southey, whose poetry he had admired from childhood but whose 'tergiversation' on political matters he intended to reproach him with: 'he to whom Bigotry, Tyranny, Law was hateful, has become the votary of those idols in a form most disgusting.' Shelley despised Southey for his support of the war in Spain, of the Church of England and of the rotten English constitution; and contrasted him with Wordsworth, who lived in poverty and integrity (and proved inaccessible). When Southey and Shelley actually met they took to one another in spite of their disagreements. Southey, at thirty-eight, convinced himself that Shelley's errors were all attributable to youth, and complacently told him that he would change as Southey himself had done. 'He will get rid of his eccentricity, and he will retain his morals, his integrity and his genius', he wrote confidently to a friend. Shelley was less certain; he admired Southey for supporting a large household of dependants, but thought him 'corrupted by the world, contaminated by Custom'.

A precious testimony of Shelley at this time was given in 1890 by a very old lady who remembered him calling on her family when she was eight:

> I think I remember best the sort of look that came upon my father's and upon Southey's face when he talked, and how I and my brother were turned out of the room.

The spoken word is often thought to be dangerous to children; and of course Shelley was interested in them, and wanted to win their minds. In January 1812 he wrote to his sister Hellen, the last member of his family of whom he had hopes, asked her about her reading and said: '*Thinking*, and thinking without letting anything but *reason* influence your mind, is the great thing.' But she never saw the letter, which was intercepted and sent to Whitton.

The general response to proclaimed atheism at this time can be judged by one of the *Tales* (1812) of a popular enough poet, Crabbe. His story tells of a country boy who reads the 'modern philosophy' in London and has to be cured of his atheism by his father, whose method is simple – he whips the 'learned boy' until he is nearly skinned. Crabbe was not regarded as an inhumane man; what lay behind such attitudes was the real dread inspired by the French Revolution, a dread which drove the English into a smug rejection of intellectual inquiry because it had proved dangerous to life and property. The older Romantic poets, Southey and Coleridge and Wordsworth, in one way and another came to minister to this smugness; it became Shelley's serious endeavour, on the other hand, to persuade people if possible that free inquiry remained good in itself and did not necessarily lead to violence.

Shelley learnt from Southey one fact that filled him with 'inconceivable emotion': that William Godwin was not, like Buffon and Voltaire and Hume, among the honourable dead, but alive and resident in London. One of his first acts in 1812 was to write to him, declare himself his disciple and beg for a meeting. Godwin's cautious response evoked a long autobiographical letter from Shelley; and the friendship, destined to become one of the oddest in English literary history, was established.

In his third letter to Godwin, Shelley announced his intention of going to Ireland to promote the cause of Catholic Emancipation: under English government the majority of the Irish people had few political or property rights, and very limited access to education or professions. Shelley's interest in the cause may well have been encouraged by the Duke of Norfolk, who was much concerned with it; but Godwin wrote nervously, suggesting that his disciple should return instead to London, fearing he was 'preparing a scene of blood'. In fact his intentions were entirely pacific.

He did not set off for Dublin at once. During January he suffered from 'nervous attacks', for which he dosed himself with laudanum, an opium-based drug taken as readily then as aspirin or tranquillizers today. Possibly the drug worked on Shelley's imagination; at all events he either imagined he was or was actually attacked at the cottage door

Robert Southey (1774–1843). Like Coleridge and Wordsworth, he abandoned his early radicalism, thereby earning Shelley's contempt

A Dublin street scene, elegance in the ascendant

one Sunday evening. A neighbour, hearing noise, came running and found him lying senseless. Harriet was at first very frightened; Shelley himself later made light of the incident. He continued the use of laudanum throughout his life.

This particular trouble was forgotten in the bustle of preparing to leave for Dublin; he hoped to observe conditions there, make contact with politicians and write and distribute pamphlets. The first of these, an *Address to the Irish People*, couched in the simplest language, urged them to patience, sobriety, hard work, religious tolerance and the avoidance of violence; and painted an idyllic picture of the good society that might evolve from such conduct, with political freedom and economic equality ensuring perfect happiness. The pamphlet was advertised, sent to leading figures, posted up in taverns and handed out in the street with Harriet's assistance.

A second pamphlet, aimed at the educated public, *Proposals for an Association*, suggested setting up an organization to work for the repeal of the Act of Union (with England) as well as for Catholic rights. Shelley spoke on this theme one evening at a public meeting in the Fishamble Street Theatre, packed with well-dressed people, for O'Connell was the first speaker. Shelley's delivery was very slow, with pauses between the sentences which allowed the audience to applaud when he attacked English oppression and hiss when he deplored religious bigotry.

His seven weeks in Dublin gave him no great opinion of its political leaders, and they had no time for him; but he was horribly impressed by the poverty which swarmed even in Sackville Street, outside his lodgings. A young widow with three infants was arrested for stealing a penny loaf before his eyes; he interceded for her but acknowledged that she was far gone in drunkenness. He was not sentimental about the brutalized Irish poor:

> Intemperance and hard labour have reduced them to machines. The oyster that is washed and driven at the mercy of the tides appears to me an animal of almost equal elevation in the scale of intellectual being.

He did not think society ready for universal suffrage, but he composed an exalted *Declaration of Rights* on the American and French patterns, and had it printed in Ireland. The conflict between his wish for radical change and his dislike of coercion emerges clearly:

> The rights of man are liberty, and an equal participation of the commonage of nature . . .
> The rights of man in the present state of society, are only to be secured by some degree of coercion to be exercised on their violator.
> The sufferer has a right that the degree of coercion employed be as slight as possible . . .
> No man has the right to disturb the public peace, by personally resisting the execution of a law however bad. He ought to acquiesce, using at the same time the utmost powers of his reason, to promote its repeal . . .
> No man has a right to do an evil thing that good may come . . .
> Expediency is inadmissible in morals. Politics are only sound when conducted on principles of morality . . .

At the same time he turned out a satirical poem, *The Devil's Walk*, whose chief merit lies in its foreshadowing of a much later one, *The Masque of Anarchy*, in certain lines:

> The hell-hounds, Murder, Want and Woe,
>   Forever hungering, flocked around;
> From Spain had Satan sought their food,
> 'Twas human woe and human blood!

Shelley was not yet a poet in achievement or even primarily in intention; he was far more interested in writing essays on political and moral themes, and he was some way through a new novel about pre-revolutionary France, *Hubert Cauvin*. (It never appeared, and the manuscript is lost.)

Before leaving Ireland in April 1812, Shelley posted off a box of his *Declaration of Rights* pamphlets to Miss Hitchener. Then he, Harriet, Eliza and an Irish servant called Dan Healy (or Hill) embarked for Wales, hoping to settle on a farm near his cousin Thomas Grove. This plan fell through for lack of money, and they moved south to Lynmouth, on the north coast of Devon, at the end of June. Here Miss Hitchener was to join them, after some hesitation and many attempts to dissuade her by her parents and the Pilfolds, all suspicious of the nature of the love Shelley was offering – had he not written to her that he regarded marriage as 'an evil of immense and extensive magnitude . . . monopolizing, exclusive, jealous'? His opinions on this subject were strongly influenced by his reading of James Lawrence's *Empire of the Nairs, or the Rights of Women, an Utopian Romance*. Lawrence, another Old Etonian, had written his book in Germany in 1793, where it was greeted as an extension of Mary Wollstonecraft's work and taken entirely seriously; but it was not translated into English until 1811. Shelley had a copy and wrote of it: 'Perfectly and decidedly do I subscribe to the truth of the principles which it is designed to establish.' The principles are that sexual constancy, even to an excellent spouse, is impossible; that the present system makes marriage a profession for ladies and prostitution the trade of less fortunate women; and that the abolition of marriage, with inheritance through the female line and children brought up by their mothers, financially supported by the state if necessary, would be a far better system. 'Let every female live perfectly uncontrolled by any man, and enjoying every freedom . . . let her choose and change her love as she please', suggested Lawrence.

Shelley's enthusiastic endorsement of Lawrence was not a passing fad; in 1814 he gave the book to his two women companions to study. Whether either Harriet or Miss Hitchener read it is not recorded. At all events his enthusiasm for Miss Hitchener was entirely intellectual and Harriet, ever ready to join him in his feelings, was as eager for her arrival as he was.

Detail from a cartoon of 1812, 'The Coronation of the Empress of the Nairs', who is seen bathing naked in approved Nair style. Cruikshank took a less enthusiastic view than Shelley

Lynmouth in 1814

Their keenness to extend their household was so great that Shelley wondered if Godwin might also be persuaded to join them; he declined, but planned a reconnaissance trip to Lynmouth for the late summer.

The remote village of Lynmouth, with its beach onto the Bristol Channel and steeply rising hills behind, delighted Shelley. The cottage was small, the landlady kind, and he began to amass a library. His two passions, for the acquisition of books and for travel, standing in direct opposition to one another, meant that 'a large share of his scanty income . . . was always expended upon books' and, as Hogg goes on to say, 'what an excellent collection of valuable books the poor poet would have owned if all his different libraries, scattered about in different localities, had been brought together under one roof'. The title of 'poet' was beginning to be appropriate. Shelley was at work on what he described modestly to his bookseller Thomas Hookham as a 'little poem' to be called *Queen Mab*.

But *Queen Mab* was set aside in June in favour of another political pamphlet, the *Letter to Lord Ellenborough*. It is a defence of the bookseller Daniel Isaac Eaton, who had been sentenced by Lord Ellenborough to

The pillory: in 1812 the
government feared the ideas of
Tom Paine enough to sentence
his publisher to this barbarous
punishment

eighteen months' imprisonment and the pillory once a month, for
publishing the third part of Tom Paine's *Age of Reason*. Eaton was a
radical and indeed a republican; his trial was a travesty, with the judge
constantly interrupting his defence. In his *Letter* Shelley pointed out
that Eaton was really on trial for holding an opinion; that there was no
necessary connection between religion and morality, and that while the
economic security of the church might be threatened by unbelievers, the
word of God should not need the protection of the law. It is heartening
to know that Eaton was cheered when brought out to the pillory,
because it was intended as a way of delivering victims over to mob
violence; people were pelted to death there in the eighteenth century.

Shelley had his pamphlet printed at the nearby town of Barnstaple
and sent copies to Hookham with instructions to show them only to
friends 'who are not informers'. He was right to be cautious, even if his
caution was a patchy thing. The government had already been
informed about the box containing his *Declaration of Rights* leaflets,
which was opened by the Customs at Holyhead. And now he took to
distributing them by a new method: he rowed out into the Bristol
Channel and sent them forth in bottles or home-made boats. Others he
launched more dramatically from the hilltop at dusk in a fire balloon.
Both exercises inspired him to sonnets:

> Bright ball of flame that through the gloom of even
> Silently takest thine aethereal way,
> And with surpassing glory dimm'st each ray
> Twinkling amid the dark blue depths of Heaven . . .

Half-way through July his fellow radical, Miss Hitchener, finally arrived to cheer them and celebrate Harriet's seventeenth and Shelley's twentieth birthdays at the beginning of August.

Shelley's next move was to send his servant Dan to Barnstaple with copies of the *Declaration of Rights* and *The Devil's Walk*, telling him to post some on buildings and hand out others to passers-by. He had taken the precaution of cutting off the printer's name, and it was this offence that led to Dan's speedy arrest. With Irish ingenuity Dan insisted that his instructions had come from a strange gentleman in black; but he was sentenced to six months' imprisonment. Shelley appealed in vain for his release but was permitted to pay fifteen shillings a week towards easing his prison conditions. Meanwhile, the town clerk wrote to the Secretary of State, Lord Sidmouth, to inform him of what had passed. The local postmaster had already sent a copy of the *Declaration* to the Secretary of the Post Office. But although Shelley had impressed the inhabitants of Devon with his activities, the Home Office advised against taking action against him. For the moment, in any case, home affairs were overshadowed by news from abroad: in August Wellington marched into Madrid, and in September Napoleon made his fatal entry into Moscow.

Shelley was unmolested, but penniless once more and obliged to borrow from his landlady Mrs Hooper, who was so taken with him that she went out to borrow more funds from her neighbours for his relief. With this, he and his three ladies left Lynmouth at the end of August, forgetting about Godwin's plan to call on them; when the philosopher arrived in September he had to find what consolation he could in hearing Mrs Hooper sing Shelley's praises. There is an envious comment by Hogg on the instant favour his friend found with the women in any household, from mistress to maid; and it is true that nobody ever thought him ordinary, partly, perhaps, because alongside the manners of a well-bred young man there was none of the usual arrogance of his class and sex. He was neither sanctimonious nor cynical, and inclined to take everyone he met seriously, an unusual experience for most women. Accounts of his physical appearance vary but agree that his hair was abundant and curly and usually in wild disorder; that his head was small, as were all his features except his eyes, which were a remarkable deep blue, 'large and animated, with a dash of wildness'; and his skin was fair and freckled. Leigh Hunt's description confirms the angelic air so many saw:

> His side-face . . . was deficient in strength, and his features would not have told well in a bust; but when fronting and looking at you attentively his aspect had a certain seraphical character that would have suited a portrait of John the Baptist or the angel whom Milton describes as holding a reed 'tipt with fire'.

The party moved first to Ilfracombe and then into Wales again, where

Tom Paine (1737–1809), one of Shelley's heroes

Tan-yr-allt, the house above the estuary

they travelled north until they reached a village exactly calculated to appeal to his interest in man's ability to reconstruct the world on a better plan than God's. William Madocks, MP, had reclaimed an area of land from the sea marshes already, built the model village of Tremadoc and established farms; he was now constructing a dyke across the estuary of the Treath Mawr river to shut out the sea further and carry a road linking Caernarvon and Merioneth. But during 1812 the sea threatened the unfinished dyke, money was running out and the project was in danger. Shelley at once promised to raise more money, at the same time offering to rent Madocks's house, Tan-yr-allt, perched in romantic isolation on the hillside above Tremadoc. Shelley's own arrest for debt in Caernarvon did not deter him; he was now accustomed to living on his future prospects and saw no reason why he should not raise money for others in the same way. The Caernarvon debt was soon settled; and he moved his party to London to find support for Madocks.

He found no one prepared to listen to his appeals. But there was something better to keep him in London, and this was the friendship of Godwin, who followed up his initial invitation to dinner with frequent meetings and lengthy talks on all aspects of Shelley's life. Godwin, now in his mid-fifties, lived very modestly with his second wife in Skinner Street, Holborn; and here Shelley and Harriet came enthusiastically and often from their rooms in Lewis's Hotel, St James's.

The Godwin household was a genuinely extraordinary one. Godwin himself had risen from quite uneducated parents through the Dissenting academies to become the foremost philosopher of his age. In 1797 he married Mary Wollstonecraft, noted for her belief in women's rights and adherence to many of the doctrines of the French Revolution, much of which she witnessed at first hand. She had brought back from France a small daughter, Fanny, by an American businessman who had deserted her. When she died giving birth to Godwin's child, another Mary, he was left with the two tiny girls; he sought a second wife, and found a neighbour, Mary Jane Clairmont, with a small son and daughter of uncertain paternity; the two forlorn groups joined forces and in due course Mr and Mrs Godwin had a son.

So there were five children to be brought up: Fanny Imlay, who seems to have assumed she was Godwin's child and certainly called herself Fanny Godwin; Charles Clairmont, a bright and enterprising boy; Mary Godwin, the cleverest; Jane Clairmont, six months younger than Mary, dark, pretty and dramatic; and small William. Charles went to a local boys' school and was found a clerkship in a publishing firm; the girls were educated mostly at home. Reading was the habit of the whole family; money was always short; Mrs Godwin worked hard at organizing a children's book publishing firm. Godwin wrote and talked.

In November 1812 Shelley met the eighteen-year-old Fanny, whom he took a great liking to, and Jane, who was a child of 14; Mary was

Mary Wollstonecraft (1759–1797), revered by Shelley; the mother of his second wife

Skinner Street, Holborn, where the Godwin family lived at no. 41, over the shop

Thomas Love Peacock
(1785–1866), poet, classicist and
satirist, whose love of Shelley did
not blind him to his
inconsistencies

away. As the Godwin friendship waxed, so poor Miss Hitchener's star waned. Harriet and Eliza Westbrook decided that she had erotic and financial designs on Shelley; he himself had suffered one of his intense revulsions, and took to calling her the Brown Demon and laughing at her behind her back. In November she was sent back to Sussex, bitterly aware that the warnings she had received from the worldly-wise were now justified, and for a while intent on pathetic attempts at vengeance. Shelley apologized, as well he might, for his inconsistent behaviour, and prepared to pay her a small annuity. Her departure was observed by Hogg, sought out by Shelley in his London chambers and drawn determinedly back into the fold. Hogg was unable to put aside his flirtatious manner with Harriet, although she had now achieved the dignity of pregnancy and was coolly cordial in return. A young poet who came into their circle in October, through Hookham, Thomas Love Peacock, was so impressed by Harriet's beauty and charm that he never lost his feeling for her and wrote her praises warmly long after her death. Certainly few brides would set themselves to learn Latin during their first pregnancy, as she did.

One further new friend was introduced to Shelley by Godwin, and this was John Newton, vegetarian and health fanatic; Shelley's own diet had been sparse since Oxford. Hogg complained bitterly about the food in his household, alleging that when he asked for pudding, Shelley answered 'a pudding is a prejudice'; and all who knew him agree that he lived largely on bread, raisins, honey, fruit and tea, and was quite regardless of mealtimes. Vegetarianism was no hardship to him and for a while he saw it as a panacea; in *Queen Mab* he even predicts that the entire animal kingdom will become herbivorous.

His new friendships and enthusiasms had not swept the thought of Tremadoc from his mind; they returned to Wales to take up residence at Tan-yr-allt, assist Madocks as far as possible, work on *Queen Mab* and embark on a course of reading under the guidance of Godwin. Plans were laid to invite Hogg and Hookham to stay in the spring. Shelley and Harriet seemed set for a happy winter, both full of a sense of purpose and cheered by a friendly letter from his father in the new year. But two political incidents disturbed him. They were the hanging of some Yorkshiremen convicted of machine-breaking, and the prison sentences passed upon Leigh Hunt and his brother for libelling the Prince Regent. Shelley suggested to Hookham raising a subscription for the children of the Luddites, and sent Leigh Hunt £20. Since Shelley made no secret of his radical views, it is possible that local disapproval of them lay behind an incident that took place on the night of 26 February – possible, though far from certain.

On that day Dan Healy returned to them from Barnstaple prison. The weather was stormy; about eleven in the evening Shelley heard a noise from his bedroom and went down with a pistol. He said he saw a man leaving through a window, who fired at him. After a struggle the man escaped, threatening revenge on the whole family. Everyone in the house now gathered in the parlour, but after a while went back to bed; at about 4 am the attacker returned and again tried to shoot

Shelley's drawing of his assailant at Tan-yr-allt

Shelley through the window. Shelley's sketch of the man makes him into a devil with horns. Some believe that the incident was arranged to frighten him; others that he hallucinated the whole affair; others again that he engineered it in order to give himself an excuse to leave the district. None of these explanations substantially alters our picture of Shelley, since we know from other evidence that he did incur hostility for his political views; that he was subject to hallucinations; and that under stress he was not always trustworthy.

As fast as they could, the Shelleys left Wales and, as they had done after the similar incident at Keswick, sailed for Dublin, summoning Hogg to join them for a holiday. But before he could arrive they had moved on to see the lakes at Killarney; and here, slightly mysteriously, Shelley and Harriet left Eliza and Dan and returned to London, where they settled in Cook's Hotel, Albemarle Street, to await the birth of their child. Hogg came on after them, and presently Eliza and Dan made their way to London also. Shelley was now busy correcting *Queen Mab* and writing notes to it. The poem was dedicated to Harriet:

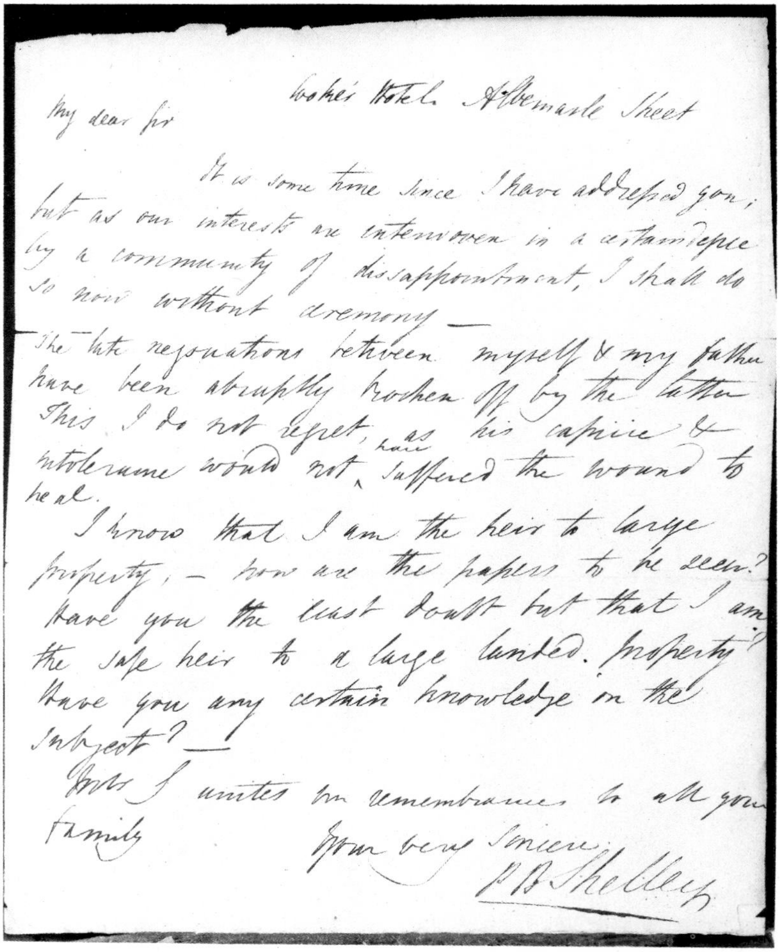

Cooke's Hotel. Albemarle Street

My dear Sir

It is some time since I have addressed you; but as our interests are interwoven in a certain degree by a community of disappointment, I shall do so now without ceremony—

The late negociations between myself & my father have been abruptly broken off by the latter. This I do not regret, as his caprice & intolerance would not have suffered the wound to heal.

I know that I am the heir to large property, — how are the papers to be seen? Have you the least doubt but that I am the safe heir to a large landed property? Have you any certain knowledge on the subject?—

Mrs S unites in remembrances to all your family

Your very Sincere

P B Shelley

Portions of an anxious letter from Shelley to his lawyer uncle, written in June 1813. Note how it has been cut and pasted up

thou wert my purer mind;
Thou wert the inspiration of my song.

She explained to a friend that although the poem was printed, 'it must not be published under pain of death, because it is too much against every existing establishment'.

It was true that Hookham would not publish for fear of prosecution, but he printed 250 copies at Shelley's expense, turning down a volume of his short poems at the same time. About seventy copies of *Queen Mab* were privately distributed. Its popularity developed only later, with radicals, for whom it became an almost sacred text, appreciating it primarily for its attitudes and arguments. It is one of the bizarre landmarks of our literature, a cross-breeding between two quite separate traditions, that of the elaborate allegorical fairy-tale and that

QUEEN MAB;

A

PHILOSOPHICAL POEM:

WITH NOTES.

BY

PERCY BYSSHE SHELLEY.

ECRASEZ L'INFAME!
Correspondance de Voltaire.

Avia Pieridum peragro loca, nullius ante
Trita solo; juvat integros accedere fonteis;
Atque haurire: juratque novos decerpere flores.
* * * * *
Unde prius nulli velarint tempora musæ.
Primum quod magnis doceo de rebus; et arctis
Religionum animos nodis exsolvere pergo.
Lucret. lib. iv.

Δος πε ςῶ, καὶ κοσμον κινησω.
Archimedes.

LONDON:
PRINTED BY P. B. SHELLEY,
23, Chapel Street, Grosvenor Square.
1813.

Title-page of *Queen Mab*. (The words of Archimedes are: 'Give me a place to stand and I shall move the whole world.')

Eight years after its appearance, Cruikshank put *Queen Mab* at the centre of his group of revolutionaries

of the historical and political polemic. The fairy queen, the sleeping girl's spirit and the magic car travelling away from the earth through space make a disconcerting start to a disquisition on the organization of society. Yet Shelley's attacks are powerful and often memorably phrased as he reveals the horrors brought by monarchy, commerce and the enslavement of labour to maintain a class of 'drones' –

> many faint with toil
> That few may know the cares and woes of sloth.

On war, religion and marriage he is equally pungent. God is shown as a projection of man's pride and cruelty, organized religion as contributing to rather than reducing human suffering, the current view of marriage and chastity as encouragement to hideous hypocrisy. And sometimes his vision has the weird splendour of his contemporary, Goya:

> Even Time, the conqueror, fled thee in his fear;
> That hoary giant, who, in lonely pride,
> So long had ruled the world, that nations fell
> Beneath his silent footstep.

Queen Mab is over two thousand lines in length, written partly in blank verse and partly in free, unrhymed lyrical sections modelled on Southey's verse. Within its odd fairy convention it progresses straightforwardly enough from a picture of the world as an 'ant-hill' full of mistakes and miseries to a vision of an ideal future. And although Shelley regarded it as a very imperfect piece of work, he maintained the intellectual positions adopted in the text and in the remarkable and lucid prose notes.

While he was working on his text, Harriet was hoping that she might be allowed to give birth to her first child at Field Place. And with the approach of his majority Shelley wrote to his father seeking a reconciliation and regretting his 'Follies' (he also ordered a large carriage for his expanding family). His father replied, but when Shelley explained that his *opinions* had not changed at all, there was an end to the exchange. On 23 June a daughter, Eliza Ianthe, was born. It is from this moment that dissension appears between Shelley and Harriet, one reason being that she did not wish to carry out his passionate wish that she should feed the baby herself. To Harriet, Eliza began to seem her ally against Shelley; and to Shelley also.

The need for economies arose again. Dan was dismissed, and the family moved thirty miles out of London to Bracknell in Berkshire, a house called High Elms belonging to Mrs Newton's sister, a Mrs Boinville, who had just lost her husband in the Russian campaign. She and her eighteen-year-old daughter Cornelia lived near by and despite their mourning were warmly welcoming neighbours. Shelley was delighted with them; he also invited Peacock to stay. Peacock was seven years older than Shelley, an even better classical scholar and a fine writer; he shared some of Shelley's prankishness but in the long run proved his most reliable and level-headed friend. Discreet, humorous and kind: of all Shelley's circle, he is the most agreeable.

Bracknell was not far enough to protect Shelley from his London creditors. The coach was packed up, Peacock agreed to accompany the family, and Shelley found a money-lender ready to lend him £500, a post-obit loan payable on his grandfather's death at a rate of 300 per cent; it had become perforce his usual way of raising money. With this they set off, first for the Lakes and then, finding no house to let there, for Edinburgh again. They did not stay long; in November they were all back in Bracknell where Shelley now made very little attempt to hide the fact that he found the company of both the Boinville ladies far more interesting than that of his wife and sister-in-law. For a short time he actually stayed in the Boinville house, taking Italian lessons with Cornelia.

Goya's giant Panic. Shelley did not know the work of Goya, but his imagination sometimes worked in the same way

Thy dewy looks sink in my breast;
Thy gentle words stir poison there;
Thou hast disturbed the only rest
That was the portion of despair!

he began an awkwardly phrased but perfectly explicit verse to her. He had earlier praised Harriet for her 'dewy' eyes also; but Harriet's dews of sympathy were for the moment dried. In March Shelley went through a second marriage ceremony with her, at St George's, Hanover Square, but this was either at her family's insistence or for technical reasons connected with raising money. She also conceived another child in March. None of this stopped her from departing with the baby Ianthe and Eliza, whom Shelley now held in abomination, for a holiday in the west country. It appears that Cornelia was removed from the scene, probably by an anxious fiancé, at the same time.

Attempts to explain Shelley's loss of love for Harriet, his own or anyone else's, tend to absurdity, since clever men can love stupid wives, unworldly men love wives who want new hats and smart clothes, short-tempered men put up with detested in-laws. Whatever Harriet's faults or virtues, Shelley was only twenty-one; what he had loved in her he loved no longer; for him, something had to change.

He fell into a state of severe dejection. 'I have sunk into a premature old age of exhaustion', he told Hogg. Mrs Boinville expressed the fear that Shelley's 'journeys after what he has never found, have racked his purse and his tranquillity'. One happy incident relieved this period. At the beginning of June Timothy Shelley was away from home, and Mrs Shelley persuaded him to make a secret visit to Field Place, his sisters, and the servants entering into the conspiracy and Shelley agreeing to wear a military uniform as a disguise. The family chattered happily together in an untidy little sitting-room they called Confusion Hall; the scene, described by a family friend, is so bright and cheerful that the sense of what Shelley was losing is brought vividly home. Within another month he was to make that loss permanent and irreparable. A new band of sisters and a new set of family troubles were to take the ascendant.

1814 is the second crisis year in Shelley's life, and the one which effectively breaks it into two parts. Not only did reconciliation with his family become impossible; he also ceased to be Godwin's disciple – though remaining a source of income to him – and largely gave up hope of being effective as a reformer, turning instead to personal mythmaking. In a sense he now set himself on the path to exile and early death, becoming the prototype of the Romantic poet in a way he had not been before, conscious that

most wretched men
Are cradled into poetry by wrong,
They learn in suffering what they teach in song.

The crisis was produced by his determination to play out his theories

Miniature of Cornelia Boinville
(1795–1877)

Below: the drawing room at Field Place, watercolour by Elizabeth Shelley

in the area of private experience, his insistence on erotic freedom as an essential part of the revolutionary programme. The discovery of the daughter of two radical thinkers – Godwin and Wollstonecraft – and the further discovery that she was prepared to disregard all the social taboos of the day for the sake of their sudden mutual attraction, acted upon him with irresistible force. Mary Godwin was a clever, pretty girl, but Harriet's rueful belief that it was the *idea* of Mary Wollstonecraft's daughter that really drew Shelley is convincing. And no part of him, in 1814 at any rate, acknowledged that he was doing anything wrong in eloping with her. Had he not just penned a reasoned justification for his behaviour?

> Constancy has nothing virtuous in itself, independently of the pleasure it confers, and partakes of the temporizing spirit of vice in proportion as it endures tamely moral defects of magnitude in the object of its indiscreet choice. . . . Persons of delicacy and virtue, unhappily united to one whom they find it impossible to love, spend the loveliest season of their life in unproductive efforts to appear otherwise than they are, for the sake of the feelings of their partner or the welfare of their mutual offspring.

The girl who precipitated Shelley's practical demonstration of the virtue of inconstancy was sixteen. She had lived her life in Skinner Street, taking lessons from her father and governesses who came to the house, with a short spell at school in Ramsgate for her health and a longer one lately with a family in Scotland. Godwin described Mary at fifteen as 'singularly bold, somewhat imperious, and active of mind'. She had grown up knowing that the people who came to the house came to discuss ideas; ideas would change the world; and ideas were more important than any of the conventional preoccupations of society.

We know that Mary revered her mother's memory, but we do not know how much she had gathered of her history and reputation in the world. Mary Wollstonecraft's objection to the economic servitude of women led her to earn her own living with great courage; her distrust of the institution of marriage meant that both her children were conceived outside it. To judge by Fanny's misery when she learned that she was not Godwin's daughter, the Godwin parents had been content to leave a good deal unsaid. Jane's paternity has not been satisfactorily sorted out to this day. Mr and Mrs Godwin formed a stable couple, and the children grew up as a normal-seeming family; only when they began to question their origins must they have become aware that each of them represented some deviation from convention. It seems likely enough that both Mary and Jane justified their readiness to enter into sexual relations with married men by what they had gathered of the theories and practice of their parents. This does not mean that they had grown worldly or sophisticated; they were not sirens, but passionate and determined innocents.

Mary and Shelley met in May and were both almost instantly bewitched. On 26 June Mary made a declaration of love to Shelley at the tomb of her mother, under the willow trees in St Pancras churchyard. He responded, and immediately addressed a poem to

her, 'Mine eyes were dim with tears unshed'. On 6 July he asked Godwin's consent for their 'union'. Godwin, who had on the same day received a large sum of money from Shelley (and was later accused by gossips of selling his daughters), 'expostulated with him with all the energy of which I was master' and thought he had dissuaded him. In fact, the lovers were simply determined to ignore Godwin's view of their case.

Shelley wrote to Harriet, who was in Bath, to tell her of his love for Mary, and Harriet came post-haste to London; she called on the Godwins and appeared distraught. She was, after all, four months advanced in pregnancy by the husband who now proposed to demote her from wife to sisterly dependant. Under pressure, Mary agreed to stop seeing Shelley. He became hysterical and arrived at Skinner Street with laudanum, a pistol and threats of suicide. He was calmed for a while but later did take a large dose of laudanum. Peacock, who had come to town at his request, found him almost unrecognizable. Harriet retreated to her father's house and Mrs Boinville came to look after him in his lodgings. He now told Mary that Harriet was involved with a Major Ryan – an instance of Shelley convincing himself of what he needed to believe – and whatever scruples Mary was holding to were overcome. In the small hours of 28 July Mary, loyally supported by Jane, both in black silk dresses, crept out of Skinner Street. Shelley was waiting with a chaise and a few pounds in his pockets; England was no longer at war with France, the Continent was open to them. In the excitement of this second elopement, he invited Jane to join the party at once. Luggageless but high-spirited, she agreed, and so a situation was set up that Mary regretted ever after. Her spirits were never again to be at the peak they had reached that June; and Shelley's belief that she was a superior being who would guide him morally and intellectually was to turn to disillusion.

Old St Pancras churchyard, where Shelley and Mary Godwin declared their love beside the grave of her mother. 'On Sunday, June 26, he accompanied Mary and her sister Jane Clairmont to the tomb of Mary's mother . . . and there, it seems, the impious idea first occurred to him of seducing her, playing the traitor to me, and deserting his wife', wrote Godwin

Dover Harbour (*above left*)
Paris, showing the Louvre, by David Cox (*left*)
A Swiss scene by Bonington (*above*)

'She was in my arms – we were safe; we were on our road to Dover.'
(Shelley)

'As we left Dover and England's white cliffs were retiring, I said to myself
I shall never see these more.' (Claire's journal)

'As soon as the Peace of 1814 had opened the Continent, he went abroad.
He visited some of the more magnificent scenes of Switzerland and
returned to England from Lucerne.' (Mary Shelley)

Reaching Dover at four in the afternoon on a day of intense heat, they found there was no channel packet until next morning. Mary, feeling ill, cooled herself in the sea and Shelley managed to hire a boat and a few sailors for immediate departure; they set sail, a squall blew up, Mary became seasick and sat between Shelley's knees while he wondered silently if they would all drown. Instead they reached Calais in the dawn and retired to a hotel, where Mrs Godwin caught up with them. She had pursued them in the hope of reclaiming Jane at least (later she said that all the daughters of the house were in love with Shelley). Jane refused her mother and Mrs Godwin returned to her depleted household. The three adventurers went on first to Boulogne and then, taking a two-wheeled cabriolet, to Paris, where the heat wave continued. The lovers spent happy sleepless nights, but Mary was also ill. They managed to see the Louvre, the Tuileries and Notre Dame and tried to call on Mary Wollstonecraft's old friend Helen Maria Williams, only to find her away. Shelley had no money left; two letters came from Hookham with reproaches but no funds; but presently a French merchant obliged, and Shelley sold his watch and chain. They set off again in the direction of Switzerland, with a donkey to carry their few bits and pieces. The donkey proving incompetent, they exchanged it at a loss for a mule on which one of the party at least might ride. Mary was still ill, Shelley sprained his ankle and soon Jane too felt unable to walk; at Troyes they sold the mule and engaged a small coach. Both girls had started to keep journals, which he sometimes wrote in too; they are one of our chief sources of knowledge about Shelley's life from now on. The other is of course his letters; and from Troyes he wrote one to Harriet, urging her to join his party in Switzerland; he also explained that he had left Peacock, currently characterized as 'expensive, inconsiderate & cold', in charge of his financial affairs.

The travellers went on through country which bore the marks of Napoleon's battles only six months before. Jane noted 'terrifcly dirty' inns in her new journal, beds impossible to sleep in, a night spent by the kitchen fire. But once over the border at Pontarlier, into Switzerland:

> the Cottages & people as if by magic became almost instantaneously clean & hospitable – The children were rosy & interesting, no sallow care worn looks – in France it is almost impossible to see a woman that looks under fifty,

wrote Jane, who believed her father to have been Swiss. After passing through Neuchâtel, they reached Brunnen on Lake Lucerne and decided to settle there for six months at least. But two days after taking an apartment Shelley and Mary freakishly decided they must return to England at once. The most urgent reason was lack of money, and, to economize, and indulge Shelley's love of water, they agreed to return by river. This involved some complicated changes of boat and cross-country journeys, and their fellow-passengers were rough company. Mary described them as 'uncleanly animals' with 'horrible and slimy faces' and Jane deplored their habits of smoking, drinking,

HISTORY

OF

A SIX WEEKS' TOUR

THROUGH

A PART OF FRANCE,
SWITZERLAND, GERMANY, AND HOLLAND:

WITH LETTERS

DESCRIPTIVE OF

A SAIL ROUND THE LAKE OF GENEVA, AND OF
THE GLACIERS OF CHAMOUNI.

LONDON:

PUBLISHED BY T. HOOKHAM, JUN.
OLD BOND STREET;

AND C. AND J. OLLIER,
WELBECK STREET.

1817.

The title-page of Mary's anonymous account of the 1814 trip, with letters and poems written by Shelley in 1816. 'Nothing can be more unpresuming than this little volume. It contains the account of some desultory visits by a party of young people . . .' (Mary's preface)

singing and 'cracking jokes of a disagreeable nature', no doubt inspired in part by the appearance of Shelley and the two girls. He entertained them by reading aloud from Mary's mother's *Letters from Sweden*, and they were all delighted by the Rhine, on whose waters Mary spent her seventeenth birthday. From Cologne they travelled by land again and embarked at Rotterdam for Gravesend, obliged to persuade the captain that he would be paid at the end of the journey. And when they reached London on 13 September, Mary and Jane sat for two hours in a coach outside Harriet's lodging while Shelley argued Harriet into providing their fares.

The pond at South End Green,
Hampstead

Another disordered and difficult winter followed. Shelley, Mary
and Jane moved from one lodging to another, mostly around Kentish
Town, pursuing wrangles with Harriet on the one hand and the
unforgiving Godwins on the other. For weeks Shelley was so threatened
by bailiffs that he could not live with his womenfolk at all; he and
Mary exchanged desperate love letters and met furtively in traditional
lovers' spots such as St Paul's. Mary was pregnant. Harriet gave
birth, a month sooner than expected, on 30 November, to Shelley's
first-born son, whom she named Charles. Neither Mrs Shelley nor
Mrs Boinville could forgive Shelley.

Peacock, however, far from being cold, was friendly and helpful.
Jane's journal notes many meals and walks in which he joined them,
to Hampstead Heath or the Primrose Hill pond where they sailed
paper and fire boats. One evening they all went to see Kean play
Hamlet but left after Act II in disgust at the poor performance.
Godwin's money troubles were persistently brought to Shelley's
attention, even though Godwin himself would speak neither to him
nor to Mary, and poor, affectionate Fanny was obliged to deliver
farcical messages. Jane and Mary kept up their reading programmes
– there was little else to occupy them in lodgings – but Shelley had no
time to write at all. 'Do you think Wordsworth could have written
such poetry, if he had ever had dealings with money lenders?' he
asked.

Fortunately his financial problems were soon to be eased; in January, old Sir Bysshe died and his father, with an eye to protecting the estates against Shelley's ruinous post-obit borrowing, settled most of his debts and granted him an annuity of £1,000 a year, £200 to go direct to Harriet.

In mid-November Hogg appeared once again and soon became a general favourite. By January he was flirting assiduously with Mary and it appears from her letters that she entertained the idea of becoming his mistress after the birth of her child. Clearly she liked him; her tone is flirtatious; but far from making this arrangement behind Shelley's back, it was done to please him and as an expression of her love for him and discipleship in the doctrines of free love: he had given her and Jane *The Empire of the Nairs* to read in September. Mary could think herself into an attitude that Harriet's timid conventionality had forbidden.

In the event, this curious piece of bravado seems to have come to nothing. Her baby was due in April; in early February they moved to lodgings in Hans Place and two weeks later the child was born there, a tiny girl. At the beginning of March they moved yet again and a few days later the baby died in the night, unnamed apparently. Shelley was also ill; a doctor told him he was consumptive, with abscesses on both lungs, and should not expect to live long. Hogg moved into the lodgings and for a while Shelley spent more time with Jane while Hogg and Mary remained very close. Shelley also visited Harriet on reasonably friendly terms several times in April. Meanwhile, Mary was pregnant again, and neither she nor Shelley seem ever to have doubted that this was his child. In April Hogg departed and from then on she was stonily uninterested in him and it was Shelley who maintained the old male friendship. If there was a crisis, centring on her jealousy of Jane and determination not to risk her own pre-eminent position with Shelley, no record of it remains.

In May she succeeded, temporarily, in ridding herself of Jane. 'Our regeneration', she wrote in her journal on the day of her departure; 'Shelley and the lady walk out . . . Shelley and his friend have a last conversation.' Mary could be sarcastic when she chose, and Jane had spent too many evenings sitting over the fire exchanging ghost stories with Shelley, too many afternoons out walking, talking and getting locked into Kensington Gardens with him, not to arouse jealousy.

She had also decided to change her name during this confused year. From now on she chose to be known as Claire (or Clara, or Clare). Only the disapproving Godwins persisted in calling her Jane; Mary simply commented: 'I wish this girl had a resolute mind.' For a while Claire stayed alone at Lynmouth, an experience she recalled later as intensely melancholy, though she was defiantly bright at the time. Shelley took Mary for a holiday in another part of the west and then left her at Clifton while he joined Peacock in his favourite Thames valley, this time at Marlow. Officially he was house-hunting; but he lingered so long that Mary's letters began to be panic-stricken and she asked if Claire were with him. Claire was not; which did not mean

that she had not already found a place in Shelley's deepest affections from which Mary's most bitter jealousy could not dislodge her.

At the end of August Mary joined him in the small furnished house he had taken at Bishopsgate, on the edge of Windsor Forest. It was the most tranquil time they had yet known. She was in mid-pregnancy, Claire was still away subsisting on money orders from Shelley and even the continuous rumblings from Godwin on the subject of his financial troubles seemed bearable for the moment. Shelley was still convinced he was dying, but his health was dramatically improved in September by a boat trip up the Thames in which Peacock, Charles Clairmont and Mary joined. The weather was brilliant; and the daily exercise of rowing and nights camping out on the river bank gave him back his strength.

At Oxford, empty for the long vacation, he showed off the sights: the Bodleian, the Clarendon Press and, as Charles noted, 'the very rooms where the two noted infidels, Shelley and Hogg' had pursued their studies. As they journeyed on upstream Shelley delightedly planned an extension to the trip which would take them into Wales by canal. But they could not muster the £20 fee for the Severn canal, and just beyond Lechlade the water became shallow, weedy and finally blocked by a herd of cattle standing right across the stream. The party stayed for two nights at the village inn in Lechlade and Shelley was

Shelley loved the river and Windsor Great Park where 'he spent his days under the oak-shades', according to Mary

Opposite page: the Thames at Great Marlow (*above*) and Lechlade (*below*)

inspired to write a churchyard meditation in which he broods on the peaceful and benevolent aspects of death rather than its charnel-house horrors:

> Here could I hope, like some inquiring child
> Sporting on graves, that death did hide from human sight
> Sweet secrets, or beside its breathless sleep
> That loveliest dreams perpetual watch did keep.

According to Mary, it was at this time that he determined to give up direct political exhortation; and when they returned to Bishopsgate he settled down to a new long poem, *Alastor, or the Spirit of Solitude*, which has none of *Queen Mab's* political insistence.

Alastor is an autobiographical fantasy – a peculiarly Shelleyan genre – in which the riverside landscape he had just been exploring is used as the setting for the journey of a young poet who dreams of an ideal love and awakes to disillusion and death. This theme allowed him to write a genuinely splendid threnody for himself, even if his persistent self-pity begs several questions:

> ah! thou hast fled!
> The brave, the gentle, and the beautiful,
> The child of grace and genius. Heartless things
> Are done and said i' the world, and many worms
> And beasts and men live on, and mighty Earth
> From sea and mountain, city and wilderness,
> In vesper low or joyous orison,
> Lifts still its solemn voice: – but thou art fled . . .

Shelley had *Alastor* printed in January 1816; John Murray declined to

Title-page of *Alastor*. Peacock suggested the name, which refers to the evil genius of solitude

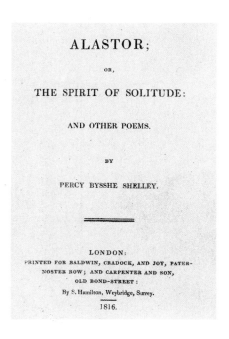

ALASTOR;

OR,

THE SPIRIT OF SOLITUDE:

AND OTHER POEMS.

BY

PERCY BYSSHE SHELLEY.

LONDON:
PRINTED FOR BALDWIN, CRADOCK, AND JOY, PATER-
NOSTER ROW; AND CARPENTER AND SON,
OLD BOND-STREET:
By S. Hamilton, Weybridge, Surrey.
1816.

The Bishopsgate cottage

publish it, but two other minor London publishers agreed to issue it jointly. Early reviews were hostile, speaking of 'sublime obscurity' and 'nonsense' and calling it 'wild and specious, untangible and incoherent as a dream'; later criticism has been more appreciative and read it as a warning against withdrawal from the world. Shelley sent a copy to Southey with a polite note, but received no acknowledgment.

Meanwhile, he had clashed with Harriet. When Charles reached his first birthday she asked for an increased allowance for the children. He countered by suggesting that she should surrender Ianthe to him and agree to a deed of separation. When she refused, Shelley threatened to withdraw her allowance altogether, a sad failure of his generous spirit.

A few weeks later he had another son. Mary gave birth to a healthy boy on 24 January; he was named William for his grandfather, despite the estrangement. Shortly afterwards Shelley wrote to Godwin complaining of his attitude: 'a young family innocent and benevolent and united, should not be confounded with prostitutes and seducers'. His feelings about England were in a bitter phase altogether, and he said he felt inclined to go abroad or live in a remote part of the country because of the 'perpetual experience of neglect or enmity from almost every one but those who are supported by my resources'. The decision to go abroad was encouraged by Claire for reasons of her own.

It was as well the Godwins were ignorant of her activities at this time. She had returned to London and, with thoughts of making a career for herself on the stage, written to Lord Byron proposing a meeting; he was supposed to have influence in the theatre. Byron, in the throes of the collapse of his marriage, was neither enthusiastic nor quite able to resist the spirited advances of a black-eyed seventeen-

Claire Clairmont (1798–1879),
Shelley's Constantia:

'In thy dark eyes a power like
  light doth lie,
Even though the sounds which
  were thy voice, which burn
Between thy lips, are laid to
  sleep . . .'

year-old. Claire managed to introduce Mary to him and spoke of
Shelley and his theories of free love. True to the spirit of the Nairs, she
proposed that he might try his luck with Mary; and he probably
gained the impression that Claire was or had been Shelley's mistress.
By the time Byron left England on 25 April Claire was pregnant by
him. She knew he was headed for Geneva, and she urged the Shelleys
in the same direction. Here both poets arrived at the end of May,
Byron accompanied by a young doctor, John Polidori, and Shelley by
Mary, the baby and Claire.

    The summer of 1816 proved cold, rainy and memorable. Outside
the Hôtel d'Angleterre at Sécheron, on the shores of Lac Léman,
Claire introduced her two poets. A real friendship sprang up between
them at once; they found they could talk together freely and at length.
They shared a disgust with the political set-up in England, and Byron
admired Shelley's scholarship and quixotic ideas, while Shelley was
impressed by Byron's brilliance and ability to reach a huge audience
with his poetry: *The Giaour, The Corsair* and the early cantos of *Childe
Harold* had already won him a European reputation. Mixed with
mutual admiration was a certain amount of disapproval and occasional backbiting; Shelley felt Byron played the aristocrat rather too
hard, and Byron would never give an opinion on Shelley's poetry.
And although each was estranged from his wife, their attitudes to
women were at variance, Shelley wanting them to be intellectual

George Gordon, Lord Byron
(1788–1824): 'I despair of rivalling
Lord Byron, and there is no other
with whom it is worth contending.'
(Shelley)

companions with whom he lived on an equal footing, Byron regarding them as diversions or pets who might obsess him for a while but were not to be taken too seriously. Byron enjoyed shocking and breaking conventions for his own purposes, but he wanted the conventions maintained; Shelley's atheism shocked him, not least, one feels, because it made his satanic poses look less terrific.

For a few weeks the pattern of their life around Lac Léman was this. Shelley and his party leased a small house, the Maison Chappuis, at Montalègre, looking across the lake to the Jura mountains, and Byron installed himself in the much grander Villa Diodati; they divided the expense of a sailing boat between them. When the long evenings were fine, both parties took to the water with pleasure; they often breakfasted together too, and spent evenings discussing poetry, magic and science. From one such evening, when all agreed to write a ghost story, came Mary's first and most celebrated work, *Frankenstein*, the story of a man-made creature driven by lack of human affection to become a murderer. Shelley's pride in Mary's work and the encouragement he gave her were fully justified by the book's success. Frankenstein's monster, if not always in the form in which Mary conceived him, has reached more people than any of the products of Byron's or Shelley's imagination. And although Mary never wrote so well again, it is proof of very remarkable ability in a girl of eighteen and, surely, a tribute to her father's educational methods.

Lac Léman at Chillon

Opposite page: Shelley's draft Will of 24 June 1816

The two parties were not without tensions. Byron found Polidori tiresome; and although he accepted Claire's furtive visits and allowed her (and Mary) to copy poetry for him, he made it clear that he did not feel any affection for her. Shelley was the one who interested him; and at the end of June, the two poets went off on their own for a week-long tour of the lake. Shelley read Rousseau's *Nouvelle Héloïse*, an account of passionate sexual and sentimental love between a well-born girl, Julie, and the tutor in her father's house, and they stopped at Meillerie and Clarens where much of the story is set. At Lausanne Byron plucked some acacia leaves in memory of Gibbon, who had finished his *Decline and Fall* there; both were struck by the horrors of Chillon's dungeon as a monument to 'cold and inhuman tyranny'. On 24 June a sudden squall and misjudgment by the boatman nearly tipped them into the lake; Byron prepared to swim and to save Shelley, who could not, but he declared his intention of going to the bottom alone rather than endangering anyone else. The boat was righted; but the incident caused Shelley that very evening to lay aside Julie's story and write his will.

Will.

To _Mary Wollstonecraft Godwin_ the whole
estates, in fee simple, ~~in fee, independ~~ & all the money in
the funds, independent of any limitations or
incumbrances, excepting the following legacies
which ~~must~~ may be paid within four years from the
time of her obtaining possession of the estate,
the interest being regularly paid in the
meantime.

Legacies

To Harriet Shelley my wife the sum of 6000
the interest of which she is to enjoy during her
life, with reversion after her death to Charles
Bysshe Shelley, my son by her.

To Charles Bysshe Shelley, in addition 5000.

To Ianthe Shelley my _daughter_ by my wife 5000

To Mary Jane Clairmont (the sister in law of
Miss Godwin) ~~~~ 12,000, one half to be laid out
in an annuity for her own life, & that of any
other person she may ~~~~ name, if she pleases to
name any other, the other half to be at her
own disposal ————
To Thomas Jefferson Hogg of the Inner Temple Esq.
2000

Had he died, Mary, William, Claire and her unborn baby would have been left to very doubtful charity. Accordingly, he named Byron and Peacock executors and bequeathed his entire inheritance to 'Mary Wollstonecraft Godwin', but for the following legacies: £6,000 to 'Harriet Shelley my wife', with £5,000 to each of her children by him; and £12,000 to Claire, half of it to go to 'any person she may name if she pleased to name any other', which is clearly a tactful way of including her coming child. The only other beneficiaries were Hogg, Byron and Peacock. Shelley's automatic assumption of responsibility for Claire and her child is proof of his acknowledgment that he was more to her than Byron could ever be, as much as of doubts concerning Byron's reliability. Later in the summer he did confront Byron with his responsibility, but it seems to have been taken for granted by both men that Shelley was in charge of Claire's life; she had, after all, described him to Byron as 'the man I have loved, and for whom I have suffered much'.

On the last day of the trip Shelley wrote his first great poem, the *Hymn to Intellectual Beauty*. Its models are the odes of Wordsworth and Coleridge, and it celebrates the spirit which visits man unpredictably, giving 'grace and truth to life's unquiet dream'. Shelley suggests that, if the spirit were not evanescent, man would be almost godlike in power; if it were never present, the world would be a place of despair. He goes on to recall his boyhood and self-dedication, and to hope, more formally, that now he is entering into maturity he will feel the spirit's effects more calmly. The *Hymn* can be read primarily, perhaps, as an account of Shelley's inner creative and psychological rhythms; technically, it shows his prodigious ability to put to use what he learnt from reading other poets.

Shelley knew he would have to return to England soon; his father's anger at his leaving the country without making proper arrangements for Harriet, Ianthe and Charles made him peremptory about the need for further discussion of money matters. To Peacock, Shelley wrote of settling in the Thames valley again and making it a 'fixed, settled, eternal home'. Meanwhile, he wanted to take a boat trip along the Danube to Constantinople and return by way of Athens, Italy and the South of France. In fact, he took Mary and Claire to Chamonix to see Mont Blanc, leaving William with a Swiss nurse named Elise. The approach to the Alps through Bonneville and along the River Arve is still dramatically beautiful, as the valley with its neat villages gives way to steep rocks, waterfalls, pines and glaciers and the sharp outlines of the Aiguille du Midi and brilliant whiteness of Mont Blanc itself appear. In the mountain hotel registers Shelley, in a fit of boyish braggadocio, inscribed himself, in Greek script, as 'democrat, great lover of mankind and atheist'. Shocked accounts were carried back to England by other tourists, a species for whom he expressed great scorn.

While in the mountains Shelley wrote a second, more difficult poem, *Mont Blanc*, in which he examines his reaction to the overwhelming landscape and asks himself how his private thoughts,

fantasies and images (Platonically placed 'in the still cave of the witch poesy') relate to 'the universe of things around'. And he suggests that the power of the universe is not a comfort-bringing power, as Wordsworth saw it, but something 'remote, serene and inaccessible', like the mountain.

The little party now retraced their steps to Montalègre and resumed their routine of reading, boating and visits to Diodati. Mary made a fire balloon and bought a telescope for Shelley's twenty-fourth birthday; a few days later a depressed letter from Fanny, saying that Mrs Godwin had told her that Shelley and Mary laughed at her, prompted them to go and buy her a watch and some books. 'Monk' Lewis, whose macabre novels and poems had so delighted Shelley, arrived to visit Byron, and both men teased the Shelleys by asserting that it was impossible to believe in ghosts without believing in God also. By now Byron had agreed to take responsibility for Claire's and his child, on the condition that she would hand it over; he wanted no more to do with her.

At the end of the month everyone at Maison Chappuis returned to England, stopping *en route* to marvel at Versailles:

The Mer de Glace at Chamonix, by Turner.

'Power dwells apart in its
    tranquillity
Remote, serene, and
    inaccessible.'
(Shelley's *Mont Blanc*)

> it seemed that the present desolation of France, the fury of the injured people, and all the horrors to which they abandoned themselves, stung by their long sufferings, flowed, naturally enough, from expenditures so immense as must have been demanded by the magnificence of this tournament. The vacant rooms of this Palace imaged well the hollow show of monarchy,

wrote Shelley in Mary's diary.

At Portsmouth they separated, Mary, Claire, William and Elise towards Bath, where Claire would await her confinement, and Shelley to London. In late September Mary joined Shelley and Peacock for a few days at Marlow and Shelley returned with her to Bath. Early in October two letters came from Fanny in which she talked interestingly of her conversations with Robert Owen about her mother, and was also clearly doing her utmost to improve relations between her sisters and the Godwins. Her third letter, posted in Bristol, alarmed Shelley, who set off at once to find her; after two unavailing visits to Bristol, news came of the suicide of an unknown young woman in a Swansea inn. This heartbreaking end to the life of Mary Wollstonecraft's beloved daughter – the very child whose existence had stayed *her* when she was tempted by suicide – was deeply felt by Shelley. He had nothing to blame himself for except the failure to notice the depth of her unhappiness and relieve it, which he would gladly have done by bringing her to live in his household. A third sister might indeed have eased the tensions between Mary and Claire; and Fanny had a special place in his imagination as the first child of a heroic radical writer and pioneer of sexual freedom. The reference in her suicide note to her 'unfortunate' birth must have struck particularly at him, living as he was with two women who had embarked on bearing children without benefit of matrimony, to a considerable degree in conscious emulation of Mary Wollstonecraft.

Shelley expressed his grief in fragmented verses. In one of these he recalls her childhood travels to Sweden with her mother:

> Thy little footsteps on the sands
> Of a remote and lonely shore –
> The twinkling of thine infant hands
> Where now the worm will feed no more.
> The laugh of mingled love & glee
> When *one* returned to gaze on thee
>
> These footsteps on the sands are fled
> Thine eyes are dark – thy hands are cold
> And she is dead – and thou art dead –

Mary put on mourning and she and Shelley determinedly pursued their reading studies. He read aloud from *Don Quixote* and *Gulliver's Travels*; to himself he read Montaigne, with much delight, and Mary re-read her mother's *Rights of Woman*, and worked at *Frankenstein*. In December he visited Leigh Hunt in London; although they had corresponded and met before, this was the start of their real friendship. But then came another horror.

On 15 December Shelley received a short letter from Hookham informing him that Harriet's drowned body had been found in the Serpentine. Shelley had had no contact with his wife since the spring, and his feelings towards her were by now detached, with a tinge of bitterness because of her threats (inspired by the Westbrooks' lawyers) to prosecute him for atheism unless he increased the allowance to the children. But this was wholly unexpected.

Her story, as far as it can be pieced out, seems to have gone like this. She had returned to her father's house with her children, but in the summer of 1816 both children were sent to the country to be cared for by a clergyman. Harriet then had a brief, presumably consolatory, love affair with an officer who was then sent abroad, leaving her pregnant. In early September she moved out of her father's house into lodgings in Hans Place, where her landlady and servant noticed her low spirits and her condition. There she lived very quietly, staying in bed a good deal; and from there, on 9 November, she left at dusk and never came back. In a letter to her sister she announced her intention of killing herself, asked forgiveness and spoke of Shelley:

> I have not written to Bysshe. Oh, no, what would it avail, my wishes or my prayers would not be attended to by him, and yet should he receive this, perhaps he might grant my request to let Ianthe remain with you always. Dear lovely child, with you she will enjoy much happiness, with him none. My dear Bysshe, let me conjure you by the remembrance of our days of happiness to grant my last wish. . . . Do not refuse my last request, I never could refuse you and if you had never left me I might have lived, but as it is I freely forgive you and may you enjoy that happiness which you have deprived me of. There is your beautiful boy, oh! be careful of him, and his love may prove one day a rich reward . . .

It is unlikely that Shelley ever saw this letter, which demonstates clearly her continued love for him.

He set off for London as soon as Hookham's letter reached him. The verdict at the inquest was simply 'found dead', and *The Times* described her as 'a respectable female far advanced in pregnancy'. Harriet's family, although they had arranged for the dragging of the Serpentine and other ponds when she disappeared, did not come forward to claim her body. She appears to have been buried under the name of Harriet Smith. Rumours that she had become a prostitute were mentioned by Shelley to Mary; to this he added vituperative blame of the Westbrooks, self-vindication and an offer of marriage to Mary, intended to make his chance of gaining custody of Harriet's children more likely. As Hunt said, this was 'soothing intelligence' to Mary. It cut no ice with Eliza Westbrook, however, who did not intend to surrender Ianthe and Charles to Shelley; for the moment they remained in Warwick.

Many of the characters in Shelley's life story are children, and Harriet Westbrook is among them. Not many schoolgirls just sixteen would have resisted such an adventure as eloping with a dazzling and sympathetic young aristocrat. His love delighted her; she gave him the passionate and naïve loyalty of a disciple in almost all his views and activities. She had no guile. If she was not very clever, and

Mary Shelley (1797–1851)

wanted to live a comfortable life, and listened too much to her sister and grew jealous, these are not very terrible faults. Her view of her time with Shelley was that it was very happy – 'the happiest and *longest* two years of my life', she wrote to a friend, meaning doubtless that they were crammed with incident. They passed like an exciting dream and thereafter her life became a nightmare. She had no resource, no strength of her own and her family did not know how to help her.

Shelley's hysterical insistence on self-justification soon quietened; and however he had come to think of her once bright hair and face, he began now to think of her end:

> The cold earth slept below
> Above the cold sky shone
> And all around
> With a chilling sound
> From caves of ice and fields of snow
> The breath of night like death did flow
> Under the sinking moon.
>
> The wintry hedge was black
> The brown grass was not seen
> The birds did rest
> In the dark thorn's breast
> Whose roots beside the pathway track
> Had bound the hard soil; and many a crack
> The black frost made between.
>
> Thine eyes glowed in the glare
> Of the departing light
> As a starry beam
> On a deep dark stream
> Shines dimly – so the moon shone there
> And it shone thru the strings of thy tangled hair
> Which shook in the blast of night.
>
> The moon made thy lips pale beloved
> The wind made thy bosom chill
> The air did shed
> On thy dear head
> Its frozen dew, and thou didst lie
> Where the bitter breath of the naked sky
> Might visit thee at will.

The Westbrooks immediately settled money on the children and claimed guardianship in the Chancery Court, offering as evidence against Shelley his letters to Harriet, *Queen Mab* and the *Letter to Lord Ellenborough*, these last two indicative of atheism and revolutionary principles deemed to unfit him for the care of children. The case took many months – during which Shelley left the country – and was finally settled to no one's satisfaction, with the children handed over to the care of a doctor of medicine, Thomas Hume, and his wife, whose plan of upbringing was judged soundly Christian and reactionary.

Shelley and Mary were married quietly at St Mildred's Church, Bread Street, on 30 December 1816. One person felt unmixed delight;

Opposite page: a copy of the Chancery Proceedings and Shelley and Mary's marriage certificate

PUBLIC RECORD OFFICE COPY.

[Pursuant to Statute 1 & 2 Vict., c. 94.]

Chancery Proceedings 1800 to 1842. Bundle 801
Shelley v. Westbrook and others.

18th January 1817
Sworn at the Public Office this Eighteenth }
day of January 1817 before me } Sewell by Utterson
Chas. Thomson.

In Chancery.

The Answer of Percy Bysshe Shelley one of the
defendants to the Bill of Complaint of Eliza Ianthe
Shelley and Charles Bysshe Shelley Infants by John
Westbrooke their Maternal Grandfather and next
Friend Complainants.

This Defendant saving and reserving to himself now and

Percy Bysshe Shelley. of the Parish
of Saint Mildred Bread Street London widower
and Mary Wollstonecraft Godwin of the City Parish
of Bath Spinster a Minor
were married in this Church by Licence with Consent of
William Godwin her Father this Thirtieth Day of
December in the Year One thousand eight hundred and Sixteen
By me Wm Heydon Curate
This Marriage was solemnized between us { Percy Bysshe Shelley.
{ Mary Wollstonecraft Godwin
In the Presence of { William Godwin
{ M J Godwin
No. 9.

this was William Godwin, who wrote to a friend: 'Mary has now . . . acquired a station and character in society.' In the evening Shelley wrote to Claire, who remained in Bath awaiting her confinement under the name of Mrs Clairmont; the secret was strictly kept from the Godwins. To his new sister-in-law he took a somewhat sarcastic tone about the ceremony 'so magical in its effects'. Shelley took Mary back to Bath and then returned to London to fight the Westbrooks. Mary joined him again at the end of January; her diary says nothing about the birth of Claire's daughter on 12 January. She was named Alba, pending Byron's wishes on the subject; but he was silent.

Shelley and Mary stayed mostly with the Hunts in Hampstead, enjoying musical parties and visits to the opera. 'I am very much pleased', wrote Mary in an unusual burst of enthusiasm after hearing Mozart's *Marriage of Figaro* for the first time. They called frequently on the now approving Godwins and met and talked with Hazlitt, who characterized Shelley as 'shrill' and did not care for him, and Keats,

'We all go to the Opera – Il Don Giovanni & the new Ballet – Le Retour du Prinptems [*sic*]. Beautiful Dancing.' (Claire's journal, 21 February 1818)

who, although friendly, felt the need to keep his distance. Just as Shelley found Byron's aristocratic assumptions galling at times, so Keats was uneasy before Shelley's social and intellectual confidence.

At this time Mary conceived her third child. The current plan was still to settle in England, and they took a twenty-one-year lease on a house in Great Marlow village on the Thames. Albion House was two stories high, with a garden, close to the river and surrounded by the lush countryside they had enjoyed already at Bishopsgate. It was also close enough to London for many visitors to come easily, and for Shelley to walk there when he wished. Peacock lived at hand, which was a joy, although Mary and he came to dislike one another. He was intensely loyal to Harriet; he was also drawn to Claire, and is said to have proposed to her; and he remained a friend in whom Shelley could confide. That winter he told Peacock as they walked in Bisham Wood that he intended to take 'a great glass of ale every night . . . to deaden my feelings'. Later he explained that the feelings concerned Harriet.

Joseph Severn's 1821 portrait of Keats

Albion House, Marlow. 'Ought we not to be happy? And so indeed we are, in spite of the Lord Chancellor', wrote Mary

Mary and Shelley travelled to Marlow at the end of February, and after staying with Peacock for a while moved into Albion House on 18 March. Claire joined them, resuming her maiden name; Alba was explained away as the child of a friend sent to the country for health reasons. Shelley ordered a piano for Claire through the musician Vincent Novello and Mary engaged a manservant and cook from London. Guests began to arrive – Godwin and the Hunts with their many children – and both Shelleys were busy writing, Mary copying and correcting *Frankenstein* and Shelley starting work on a long narrative poem to be called *Laon and Cythna; or, The Revolution of the Golden City: A Vision of the Nineteenth Century*.

Shelley's aim in this poem, which runs to twelve cantos and nearly five thousand lines, is more interesting than his achievement. He chose to write in Spenserian stanzas, 'enticed by the brilliance and magnificence of sound which a mind that has been nourished upon musical thoughts can produce'. Modestly he explains that blank verse gives 'no shelter for mediocrity'. But, he adds, he has written fearlessly; the poem is not didactic but narrative; its theme is intended, however, to revive enthusiasm for reform and revolution after the panic responses to the French Revolution. 'Methinks, those who now live have survived an age of despair', he writes in the preface:

Two sketches by Shelley, the lower drawn on the back of the fragment addressed to Fanny Imlay and possibly representing steps leading to a grave

many of the most ardent and tender-hearted of the worshippers of public good have been morally ruined by what a partial glimpse of the events they deplored appeared to show as the melancholy desolation of all their cherished hopes.

Shelley was striving to answer the apostasy of the Lake Poets, and of course many more. The aim was interesting and admirable; it involved a sympathetic delineation of a feminist leader and a determined presentation of erotic freedom as part of the revolutionary programme. Indeed, as Shelley first wrote the poem *Laon and Cythna*, the two revolutionary leaders were brother and sister who became lovers. The incest was intended to shock the reader in much the same way as later surrealist techniques; possibly the theme and the technique both owed something to Shelley's talks with Byron. The actual narrative includes an allegorical eagle and serpent, several boat voyages, the imprisonment and temporary madness of both hero and heroine (during hers she gives birth to a child as a result of rape, and the child is taken from her), battle scenes in which the virtuous revolutionary adherents of Laon refuse to fight and are swiftly overcome, a sexual idyll between hero and heroine in a rural retreat, while famine and pestilence ravage the world, and their incineration together on a huge pyre, to which both voluntarily submit and from which they 'awake' to find themselves in yet another boat travelling to paradise. Even Hunt, now Shelley's warmest champion, felt obliged to say in his review that the poem could not possibly become popular, and blamed its author for obscurity and repetitive imagery 'too drawn from the elements, particularly the sea'.

A tiny first edition was quickly withdrawn, and Shelley's new publisher, Charles Ollier, a friend of Hunt, insisted on removing the brother and sister relation of Laon and Cythna; the poem was also retitled *The Revolt of Islam*. It remains a difficult text ideologically, since it prophesies a revolution that fails for lack of physical force and is also determinedly pacifist in its stance: Laon and Cythna are both willing martyrs, not the stuff of Marxist activists.

As Shelley started work on the poem in March 1817, he published another prose pamphlet, *A Proposal for Putting Reform to the Vote*. It was signed 'by the Hermit of Marlow' and copies were sent to well-known reformers. Shelley was proposing a referendum, to be organized by those interested in reform, not immediate universal suffrage. He stated his agreement with Paine that a republic is the best form of government but considered that humanity was still too childish to do away with such toys as monarchy and aristocracy. Little notice was taken of the Hermit's proposals, and none of his and Peacock's resolve to refuse to pay their taxes, following Hampden's principle. His good intentions had to find their outlet in ministering to the poor around Marlow; here there was plenty of scope, for the local industry of lace-making was severely hit by the hard times and many were going hungry. Witnesses to Shelley's generosity in providing blankets, food and other necessaries are matched by memories of the well-to-do of the district, who thought he was mad.

The *Examiner* defends Shelley against the *Quarterly*, 26 September 1819

Frankenstein was finished in May. Claire was also writing a novel – it was judged bad, and has disappeared – and practising her singing and piano playing, which inspired Shelley to a famous lyric, *To Constantia, Singing*. It was not shown to Mary but sent to the *Oxford Herald* to be published under the pseudonym 'Pleyel'. From March to September Shelley was working on *Laon and Cythna*. He did a good deal of writing outside, on the river or beside it, as he told in the fine dedicatory stanzas to Mary ('mine own heart's home'). Otherwise Hunt, Hogg and Peacock were his occasional companions and with one of these he would sometimes walk to London. In late May he made the trip by boat with Mary; they went eagerly to the opera now, but he was still a reluctant theatre-goer and when Peacock made him attend a performance of Sheridan's *School for Scandal* he protested, 'I see the purpose of this comedy. It is to associate virtue with bottles and glasses, and villany with books.'

This was the summer in which, according to Peacock, Shelley's hypochondriacal fancies led him to believe he was developing elephantiasis after sitting next to a woman with fat legs on a coach; for some weeks he subjected his legs to regular and anxious scrutiny. This passed, but in July he began to feel generally unwell. In September William and Alba – both cared for by Elise – were joined by a third baby, Shelley and Mary's daughter. 'It is called Clara', he noted in a letter to Byron, to whom he also spoke of being threatened with a speedy death unless he travelled to a warm climate. By December he was telling Godwin that he was consumptive and swinging between a sort of deadly torpor and a state of 'such unnatural and keen excitement that . . . I find the very blades of grass and the boughs of distant trees present themselves to me with microscopical distinctness'. Albion House, so charming in the spring and summer, was now dark and cold. He caught an eye infection during his visits to the poor. Money problems began to press again; Godwin's demands were endless, and Shelley was arrested for debt, on his uncle Pilfold's instructions, when he was in London in October.

Most of November was spent in lodgings off the Euston Road where Mary and Claire came to join him alternately, the other remaining with the children at Marlow. And now Shelley wrote his second 'Hermit of Marlow' pamphlet, a most elegant political polemic, *An Address to the People on the Death of Princess Charlotte*.

The princess, daughter of the Prince Regent, died in childbirth on 6 November, to general dismay. She was popular and she was in the direct line of succession – her death brought Victoria to the throne in due course. The day after her death three labourers were hanged and beheaded at Derby for their part in an insurrectionary march to which they had been at least partially incited by an *agent provocateur*.

Memorial card published on the occasion of the death of Princess Charlotte

SACRED TO THE MEMORY
of her Royal Highness
THE PRINCESS CHARLOTTE OF WALES AND SAXE COBOURG
who died Nov.r 6.th 1817 Aged 21 Y.rs 10 M.s

And is she gone! the nations hope and joy,   Yes she is gone! her soul to heaven is fled,
O what a cause for sorrow and for gloom,   And there she dwells enthron'd in bliss above.
The Princess and her royal infant boy,   She whose example such a radiance shed,
By deaths cold hand are hurried to the tomb.   Of splendid virtue and domestic love.

London Published Nov.r 20.th 1817 by R. Miller, 24 Old Fish St.

Allegra (1817–1822), daughter of
Claire Clairmont and Lord Byron

This uprising had given the government the chance to make a fearful
example to any other would-be insurrectionaries. It also united
radicals and reformers in opposition to government policy. Shelley's
pamphlet is written with vigour and feeling, from the beginning
where he invokes Paine's famous remark about pitying the plumage
but forgetting the dying bird (itself an answer to Burke's lament for
Marie Antoinette) to the peroration where he mourns the corpse of
British liberty.

England was in an unhappy state; but Shelley's departure in 1818,
after which he never returned, was made for entirely personal reasons.
First his health, which had become bad enough to alarm Mary and
for which the doctors recommended a warm climate. Then his sense
of persecution, which included the fear that even his children by Mary
might be taken from him, and that he was hated and ostracized.
Although this is hardly borne out by the record of his visits during
his last months in England, it is clearly what he felt, and he
dramatized the feeling in the narrative poem *Rosalind and Helen*, which
describes the loneliness of two women whose beliefs and behaviour
have made them outcasts. It is true too that all communication with
his father, mother and sisters was now at an end. His new in-laws
were not much comfort; both Shelley and Mary undoubtedly wanted
to put the sea between themselves and Godwin's eternal cry for
money. Next was the question of Alba, now christened Clara Allegra
by Byron's wish. Shelley felt he must hand her over to Byron, both
for her own sake and in order to end rumours of a Shelley harem.

The passage of
Mont Cenis by
Turner

Since Byron showed no sign of fetching her, they must take her to him. Finally, both Mary and Shelley enjoyed travel for its own sake and wanted to make a conscientious inspection of the cities, landscapes and antiquities of Italy: to find inspiration as well as a warm climate, tolerance and cheap living.

For this he was giving up the prospect of visits to Ianthe and Charles and of forming any sort of friendship with their guardians. He was also diminishing his already slender chance of finding an audience for his political statements; no more were published in his lifetime, nor was he in a position to urge Hunt or Ollier to risk prosecution on his behalf while he remained abroad. But he was in no mood for weighing pros and cons.

He set off in excellent spirits. 'Motion always has this effect upon the blood, even when the mind knows that there are causes for dejection', he wrote to Hunt from Calais. He was twenty-five and had four women and three babies in his charge. Mary at twenty with two, Claire still nineteen with one, and the two maids, little Milly Shields from Marlow and the older Elise, looking forward to seeing her own illegitimate daughter Aimée on the journey through Savoy. In terms of sheer organizing ability required, and fatigue, Shelley's journeys command admiration, particularly when one thinks of the state of the roads, the inns and transport available This time there was no question of mules or boats. A carriage was bought at Calais and they went rapidly south, avoiding Paris and going through Dijon and Lyons, where there was just time to go to the theatre; and on due east into the Alps.

At the Savoy border Shelley's books aroused the suspicions of the Customs officers and were sent off to be examined by the censor, a priest; Savoy was in the throes of reversing the twenty years of reform brought by the free-thinking French, and the same was true of Italy, over which Count Metternich had set Austria in 1815 as a well-armed, tyrannical watchdog. But Shelley's books were returned; the party stopped at Chambéry and then took the road over Mont Cenis. He sang through the passes, and joked that the mountains were God's *corps de ballet*, and they all blessed Napoleon for his good new road. As they descended to Susa the snow gave way to primroses and Claire noted euphorically 'a sky without a cloud – everything bright and serene – the cloudless sky of Italy – the bright & the beautiful'. At Turin they went to the opera; on 4 April they were in Milan, where they enjoyed a 'most magnificent ballet Pantomime of Othello' and the snowy pinnacles of the cathedral.

At first, Shelley thought of taking a house on Como and inviting Byron for a second lakeside summer. He and Mary set off to look for one, viewed several but failed to settle on any; and Shelley got into trouble with the police for walking about the countryside with his pistols. In any case Byron was not interested, despite Shelley's most charming and reasonable persuasions. It was decided at last that Elise should go with Allegra to Venice at the end of the month.

Milan Cathedral: 'I can conceive of no building that partakes more perfectly of the nature of air & heaven.' (Claire's journal)

Shelley distracted Claire from her grief with nightly games of chess in the week before the departure, and then immediately carried her and the rest of the party off south over the Apennines to Pisa. He had written to Byron, 'You will find your little Allegra quite well. I think she is the most lovely and engaging child I ever beheld.' Characteristically, he did not except his own children.

The question has to be asked whether at this time, in the process of consoling Claire for her loss, Shelley himself impregnated her with a child, to be born at the end of the year in Naples. Most Shelley scholars reject the idea that this child was Claire's although Elise testified that she was. In its favour is the undoubted fact that Shelley and Claire loved one another and that there was nothing in the principle of either to rule out the natural expression of their love. Shelley himself seems to have been devoid of sexual jealousy and hoped to educate his womenfolk into an equally easy frame of mind. He asserted more than once that the giving of love to one person need not mean the withholding from all others; and Claire was his disciple, believed in sexual freedom for women, had loved him before becoming Byron's mistress and was now triply bound to him by gratitude, grief and shared experience and beliefs. (Moreover there is evidence that Shelley thought he knew something about birth control, to which he refers in a notebook.) The events of Shelley's household in 1818 take on a different aspect as one accepts or rejects this thesis, to which we shall have to return.

Outwardly, what happened was as follows. For the first week of May they journeyed to Pisa, 'a large disagreeable city almost without inhabitants', Shelley wrote to Peacock; and to Godwin he commented that 'the modern Italians seem a miserable people – without sensibility or imagination or understanding'. At Pisa they heard from Elise that she had reached Venice safely with Allegra. They then travelled on to Leghorn, where they had a letter of introduction to a Mrs Gisborne. Maria Gisborne, as a very young matron, had looked after Mary in her infancy on the death of her mother; widowed herself soon after, she turned down a proposal of marriage from Godwin. She had lived for many years in Italy with her son Henry Reveley, now about thirty and an engineer, and her second husband, a retired businessman whom the Shelleys were inclined to mock but who became one of the people Shelley felt able to confide in.

An immediate, warm friendship sprang up between the two groups, tempting Shelley to stay for longer than they had meant in Leghorn; but at the end of May increasing heat sent them up into the hills. They rented a house, Casa Bertini, in the chestnut woods around Bagni di Lucca, and settled down to a quiet life, looked after by Italian servants. One of these, the factotum Paolo Foggi, was to play a villainous part, but for the moment things seemed peaceful enough. Shelley set to translating Plato's *Symposium*, always neglected in England on account of its acceptance of homosexual love, which Shelley dealt with delicately but fairly. Mary was copying *Rosalind and Helen*. (The laborious work of making fair copies was the traditional voluntary occupation of wives and mistresses; as far as we know Shelley copied only a few pages of *Frankenstein* for Mary.)

He was pleased with the climate, the fine hot weather, the clouds and the stars. He took his women horse riding (Claire fell off twice) and found himself a forest stream beside which he could sit naked on the rocks reading before clambering in its pools and waterfalls. His travel letters are superb; Peacock was the chief recipient, and had agreed to have regular boxes of books sent from London. One promised now was his newly published novel *Nightmare Abbey*, in which the character of Scythrop is at any rate an allusion to Shelley in that he is at loggerheads with his father, has plans for reforming the world and is torn between two young women, both of whom he loves, but both of whom he loses. The satire was too mild to offend, though it was not calculated to please Mary, who took her stand by protesting that Shelley, unlike Scythrop, did not take wine. Her own novel, *Frankenstein*, was receiving good reviews.

Shelley's intention was to move his party to Florence in September; but before that Claire persuaded him to something different. She expressed a determination to visit Allegra; and if she was pregnant, she had an additional motive for going away with Shelley. On 17 August she and he set off, accompanied by Paolo as far as Florence, for Venice. Mary, disconsolate at being left, summoned the Gisbornes to stay with her. Shelley wrote consolingly from Florence:

> the most beautiful city I ever saw. It is surrounded with cultivated hills & from the bridge which crosses the broad channel of the Arno, the view is the most animated & elegant I ever saw. You see three or four bridges – one apparently supported by Corinthian pillars, & the white sails of the boats relieved by the deep green of the forest which comes to the waters edge, & the sloping hills covered with bright villas on every side. Domes & steeples rise on all sides & the cleanliness is remarkably great. – On the other side there are the foldings of the Vale of Arno above, first the hills of olive and vine, then the chestnut woods, & then the blue & misty pine forests which invest the aerial Apennines that fade in the distance.

From Padua, where Claire originally intended to stay but then changed her mind, they travelled on by gondola. Arriving in Venice, they went straight to the Hoppners (Hoppner was the British consul-general at Venice, with a Swiss wife, and they had agreed to look after Allegra for Byron). Shelley left Claire with them and Elise and

Allegra – taller, paler, less lively – and went to Byron, who carried him off across the lagoon to the Lido, not a site for luxury hotels but then

> a bare strand
> Of hillocks, heaped from ever-shifting sand,
> Matted with thistles and amphibious weeds,
> Such as from earth's embrace the salt ooze breeds,
> Is this; an uninhabited sea-side,
> Which the lone fisher, when his nets are dried,
> Abandons; and no other object breaks
> The waste, but one dwarf tree and some few stakes
> Broken and unrepaired, and the tide makes
> A narrow space of level sand thereon . . .

Byron had horses waiting, and the two men rode along the beach; 'our conversation', wrote Shelley, 'consisted in histories of his wounded feelings, & questions as to my affairs, & great professions of friendship & regard for me'. They talked too of literary matters, Byron reciting parts of *Childe Harold*.

Byron's proposal was that Shelley should take Claire and Allegra to a villa he leased at Este, beyond Padua (where he believed Mary and the children were), and enjoy the opportunity of seeing Venice. After some uncertainty Shelley summoned Mary, who packed up obediently and set off with the two children and Paolo again in attendance, arriving at Este on 5 September. The villa was called I Capuccini and Mary described it in her notes to Shelley's poems many years later:

> I Capuccini was a villa built on the site of a Capuchin convent, demolished when the French suppressed religious houses; it was situated on the very overhanging brow of a low hill at the foot of a range of higher ones. The house was cheerful and pleasant; a vine-trellised walk . . . led from the hall-door to a summer-house at the end of the garden, which Shelley made his study, and in which he began the *Prometheus*; and here also, as he mentions in a letter, he wrote *Julian and Maddalo*.

A propitious place, it seemed, even though Claire's health obliged her to make frequent visits to the doctor in Padua, and Shelley was eager to return to Venice to be with Byron. Mary agreed to go with him, bringing baby Clara, who had been unwell but now seemed better. On the way to Venice she grew obviously ill; at Fusina the Austrian soldiers stopped them, demanding passports which they had forgotten. Shelley overcame their objections and they crossed the lagoon with the distressed baby. Mary waited in the hall of an inn while he went to find a doctor; and in the hall of the inn Clara died. The Hoppners instantly insisted on taking Mary and Shelley into their house; and for several days they dutifully saw the sights of Venice. Clara was buried on the Lido beach, with no memorial stone.

All their lives, both Mary and Shelley were subject to periods of depression; the breakdown of confidence and good relations between them at this time made these much more acute. There can be no doubt that she blamed him for the death of Clara, and that his readiness to act at Claire's bidding rather than consider her and her children first was a good part of the cause of her anger and misery.

This is a familiar enough pattern, the benevolent man whose benevolence towards the world outside his family enrages his wife. Whether Mary's anger took the form of coldness only or outbursts of accusing talk, it distressed Shelley without changing him. He decided that Mary must be shielded by being kept in ignorance of whatever upset her. He was still deeply affectionate, but she was no longer his perfect mate and certainly no longer the pattern of female excellence, free, independent and above jealousy. Mary now exhibited every sign of conventional wifely behaviour; and as she grew more careful and respectable, Claire's dash and open-mindedness contrasted all the more. In defence of Mary, it must be said that the position of wife tends to produce wifely behaviour.

Out of his dejection, Shelley began to make some of his finest poetry. The easy assurance of *Julian and Maddalo* throughout its dramatic narrative, which incorporates the Venetian setting, the figures of Byron, Shelley, Allegra and a mysterious madman confined to the lagoon asylum, who has been cruelly used by a beloved but hysterically destructive woman, represents another technical advance in his work and shows too how supremely well he wrote when tied to

Venice, the Lido.

'. . . the town is silent, one may write
Or read in gondolas by day or night,
Having the little brazen lamp alight,
Unseen, uninterrupted . . .'
(*Julian and Maddalo*)

the real world and actual experience. Although he sent a copy to Hunt, discussed publication with Ollier, and planned to write matching poems in which other Italian cities would provide the backcloths for stories 'drawn from dreadful or beautiful realities', he received no encouragement. Incredibly, *Julian and Maddalo* was not published until after his death. The less interesting *Lines written among the Euganean Hills* was, perhaps because of its glittering descriptions of Venice:

> Column, tower, and dome, and spire,
> Shine like obelisks of fire,
> Pointing with inconstant motion
> From the altar of dark ocean
> To the sapphire-tinted skies . . .

It is a meditative poem, predicting Venice's ultimate sinking beneath the water and lamenting its political servitude to the Austrians. It also extends rather formal congratulations to the city for sheltering Byron ('tempest-cleaving Swan / Of the songs of Albion') and ends with a description of Shelley's familiar paradisal vision, a 'calm and blooming cove', reached by boat, within sound of the sea, surrounded by grass, flowers and forests – a vision so powerful that it has become the staple of what twentieth-century tourists seek in their restless hordes.

In November these more innocent tourists set off south again, through Ferrara with its memorials of Ariosto and Tasso, their manuscripts in the library and the cell where Tasso was incarcerated in his madness for seven years. Shelley prised a fragment of wood from the cell door to send to Peacock; Tasso, the mad, persecuted genius, was an obvious hero and Shelley had plans to write a play about him. Then on to Bologna and Spoleto, 'the most romantic city I ever saw', with its Roman aqueduct and orange groves hung with golden fruit at this season. 'Behold me in the capital of the vanished world', began his first letter from Rome; but they passed rapidly through, intending to view it in the spring. He was pleased in passing by the Customs House, built in the ruins of a temple to Antoninus Pius:

> the Corinthian columns rise over the dwindled palaces of the modern town, & the wrought cornice is changed on one side as it were to masses of wave worn precipice which overhangs you far far on high.

He also had time to notice the English burying place where so soon one of his children and then he himself would lie:

> a green slope near the walls, under the pyramidal tomb of Cestius . . . I think the most beautiful & solemn cemetery I ever beheld. To see the sun shining on its bright grass fresh when we visited it with the autumnal dews, & hear the whispering of the wind among the leaves of the trees which have overgrown the tomb of Cestius, & the coil which is stirring in the sunwarm earth & to mark the tombs mostly of women and young people who were buried there, one might, if one were to die, desire the sleep they seem to sleep. Such is the human mind & so it peoples with its wishes vacancy & oblivion.

He travelled ahead of the others to find suitable lodgings in Naples, in the Riviera di Chiaia. When they arrived a few days later earnest sightseeing began, including an ascent of Vesuvius, with Mary and Shelley on mules and Claire carried in a chair; a boat trip across the bay of Baiae and an expedition to Pompeii. These were well-established tourist attractions – he may have recalled his father's Vesuvius print, trophy of the Grand Tour – but Shelley was in no frame of mind to respond to them conventionally. Most of his best short poems are melancholy; the *Stanzas written in Dejection, near Naples* are a bitter expression of grinding discontent. After describing the warmth and beauty of the scene about him, he says:

> Alas! I have nor hope nor health,
>   Nor peace within nor calm around,
> Nor that content surpassing wealth
>   The sage in meditation found,
>   And walked with inward glory crowned –
> Nor fame, nor power, nor love, nor leisure.
>   Others I see whom these surround –
> Smiling they live, and call life pleasure; –
> To me that cup has been dealt in another measure.

Bologna: 'there are two towers here one 400 foot high ugly things built of brick, which lean both different ways, & with the delusion of moonlight shadows you almost fancy the city is rocked by an earthquake.' (Shelley to Peacock)

The poem was dated December 1818. Mary Shelley attributed the dejection to physical ill health (Shelley's symptoms of acute, spasmodic pain throughout the Italian years suggest he suffered from kidney stones). Another reason put forward is the death of Clara; but, in fact, Shelley seems not to have formed close attachments to his children until they were past babyhood. A fragment in a later notebook speaks of having had 'two babes – a sister and a brother / Death has the one – the Chancellor the other'; and since these must be Ianthe and William, the implication is that neither Mary's premature daughter, nor Clara, nor Charles, inhabited his imagination as the older children did.

Yet another baby now appears on the scene. In February (1819) Shelley registered the birth of a daughter, Elena Adelaide Shelley, giving her birthday as 27 December, the place his lodgings in Naples. He named himself as father and Mary as mother; contrary to custom, she was not present at the registration, but a midwife was. Mary's journal makes no mention of this child, but notes that Claire was unwell on the 27th. Elena is of course the child later attributed by Elise to Claire and Shelley in her talk with the Hoppners in 1820. It has been suggested that she was a foundling 'adopted' by Shelley in order to cheer Mary: hardly credible, since she was never taken into the household. In any case it would have been unnecessary to falsify her registration for such a purpose. Another suggestion, that she was Elise's child by Shelley, makes no better sense. Every theory has drawbacks, but the least implausible case remains that she was Claire's and Shelley's, a seven-month baby who found them unprepared and was perhaps not expected to live. The absence of Claire's journal during the months in which she would have been pregnant is significant because she marked her periods regularly with a cross; there is no record between April 1818 and March 1819. Finally, Shelley's exhausted despair becomes wholly understandable.

A fragment of Claire's journal, Milan

82

At this date, proof is unlikely (although Elena's existence was uncovered only in 1936 by the American scholar Newman Ivey White), but one argument runs like this: realizing that Clara's death and Mary's jealousy made it inconceivable that she would accept Claire's child, Shelley had to persuade Claire to put the baby to foster-parents, with a promise that they would recover her when possible. Claire, panicked by the early arrival, must then have agreed; the birth of a mysterious second child to her would fatally weaken her bargaining position with Byron, and Allegra, whom she had nursed for the first fifteen months of her life, must have the greater claim.

Some bitter and enigmatic remarks in Claire's later notebooks are explained, and the first 'official' biographer Dowden's destruction of some pages. Shelley's and Mary's denials never looked very convincing, not least because they omitted to mention Elena's existence. The biggest stumbling-block remains whether we can believe that Shelley and Claire would have handed over their child. The answer to this is that it may have appeared the only possible course. Claire had to choose between that or keeping the child alone in a foreign country, separating from Shelley and losing the possibility of seeing Allegra again. Shelley had either to alienate Mary permanently or to temporize.

During this period Paolo and Elise were both discharged; according to Mary, she discovered that Elise was pregnant by Paolo and, rather surprisingly, thought it best for her to marry him. No more is heard of this pregnancy, though plenty of the Foggis. Shelley's last act in Naples was to register Elena, on 27 February. In Mary's diary for the next day, as they journeyed away, are the words 'A most tremendous fuss'; possibly made by Claire.

Shelley's letters to Peacock and Hogg are entirely devoted to descriptions of scenery and artistic treasures, including Michelangelo's study for the Sistine Chapel, which he heartily disliked – 'a kind of Titus Andronicus in painting' – largely on account of its Christian inspiration and God's evident enjoyment of 'the final scene of the infernal tragedy he set the Universe to act'. Shelley was about to present Jupiter, in his *Prometheus Unbound*, very much in this guise; his 'antique empire' upheld by faith and fear, but assailed by the soul of doubting and reproachful man. The first act of *Prometheus*, written at I Capuccini, had been laid aside during the difficult months in Naples; in Rome it was taken up again.

The intention was to return to Naples at the end of May for a further six months' visit. Meanwhile, Rome spread its consolations before them. Shelley took passionate delight in the ruined baths of Caracalla, its huge arches and Piranesi-like stairways leading to the sky, covered with self-sown flowers and blossoming shrubs; here he sat and worked on *Prometheus*. There was some social life of a conventional kind, evening parties and conversazioni at the Signora Dionigi's, an elderly bluestocking who assembled curious gatherings of cardinals and elegant, tongue-tied English gentlemen. There were drives through the Borghese gardens, landscaped in the English style;

paintings to inspect – seventeenth-century ones, by Guido Reni and Domenichino, impressed them – and all the great mixture of modern, Renaissance and antique to survey. Under Shelley's tuition the Pantheon was duly preferred to St Peter's, and there were walks to the Campidoglio, the Forum and the Colosseum. Claire was taking singing lessons seriously; in May she discreetly noted in her journal that Mary was pregnant again. The arrival of Amelia Curran, daughter of the Irish politician, gave them another interest; she had come to study painting, and immediately embarked on portraits of Claire, Shelley and little William.

But on 25 May William became ill. He was watched over with agonizing love by Shelley, Mary and Claire; on 7 June he died. All three were utterly reduced; the two women abandoned their journals and Mary wrote to Marianne Hunt, 'I feel that I am not fit for anything and therefore not fit to live'. And on Shelley's birthday in August – they had left Rome, not for Naples but for Leghorn – she took up her diary again with an entry cruelly summing up her experience:

> We have now lived five years together; and if all the events of the five years were blotted out, I might be happy; but to have won, and then cruelly to have lost, the associations of four years is not an accident to which the human mind can bend without much suffering.

But Shelley possessed what Mary did not: a spirit that renewed itself, or, at worst, continued to sing even in despair. He had streaks of

Guido Reni's Beatrice Cenci

self-hatred, the bitter self-hatred of the idealist and experimenter with life who sees his experiments fail but cannot become a comfortable apostate. He had suicidal leanings. The lines

> Bright reason will mock thee
> Like the sun from a wintry sky

express perfectly his wincing reaction to the condemnation of people of good sense. He suffered, at not always finding a publisher, at not finding a public, at being simultaneously confined and exiled. During the last three and a half years of his life one feels him struggling to escape – to the East, to England, into love, to the grave; and his poems chiefly celebrate disillusion, or when they dwell on the good in the world, it is to express the impossibility of holding to more than 'one moment's good'. Yet, as he said in his *Defence of Poetry*, 'the great instrument of moral good is the imagination', and he continued to serve his ideals. He worked on; and the poems of his despair speak to us with a still clearer voice than the poems of his hopes.

They took their wounds to the Gisbornes and then found a house near them, outside Leghorn. The Villa Valsovano had a roof-top terrace which Shelley took as his study and sometimes called Scythrop's tower, in compliment to Peacock's mocking vision; and here he sat working, mostly on a play that Mary had urged him to attempt. The subject was Beatrice Cenci, a Roman heroine driven by her father's atrocious villainy to murder him. *The Cenci* is the only one

Charles Clairmont

of his works that he discussed with Mary as he wrote; and while it achieved more success than the others during his lifetime, which was what she very reasonably wanted for him, it reads as a very academic exercise today. As he said in his dedication to Hunt, he has laid aside his own visions; there is little of his spirit in it, and none of his experience of life, but an overpowering flavour of Shakespearean pastiche and curiously wooden horror.

More pleasantly, he took up the study of Spanish with Mrs Gisborne; and when Charles Clairmont arrived in September on his way from Spain to Vienna, he joined in the Spanish reading. The study of a new language was always vivifying to Shelley; his quickness and astonishing memory enabled him to read them very rapidly; and when his own writing was not going well, he turned to translation for mental exercise, as now to Calderón.

Early in September news came from England that rekindled his political fires. On 16 August a cheerful and orderly assembly of eighty thousand working men and women with their children, clad in their Sunday best, carrying banners and accompanied by bands, met in the fields of Peterloo outside Manchester to hear an address on parliamentary reform. The occasion was peaceful until the militia was set on them, injuring over four hundred and killing nine. The massacre aroused incredulous indignation, and the apprehension of the government. When Shelley heard of it, he was spurred to write a series of political poems in the popular style he had attempted in Dublin. His hope was that they would be published in England to act as street songs, inspirations to the people. *The Masque of Anarchy* is deservedly the most famous, from its apocalyptic beginning –

> As I lay asleep in Italy
> There came a voice from over the Sea,
> And with great power it forth led me
> To walk in the visions of Poesy.
>
> I met Murder on the way –
> He had a mask like Castlereagh –
> Very smooth he looked, yet grim;
> Seven bloodhounds followed him:
>
> All were fat; and well they might
> Be in admirable plight,
> For one by one, and two by two,
> He tossed them human hearts to chew
> Which from his wide cloak he drew.

– to its decidedly equivocal last stanzas where, after advocating passive resistance ('Look upon them as they slay / Till their rage had died away') he finishes:

> Rise like Lions after slumber
> In unvanquishable number –
> Shake your chains to earth like dew
> Which in sleep had fallen on you –
> Ye are many – they are few.

'The Massacre of Peterloo or a Specimen of English Liberty'

DISPERSAL OF THE REFORM MEETING AT MANCHESTER BY A MILITARY FORCE.

[*From the Times.*]

This meeting, which has caused such universal anxiety and trepidation throughout the whole of the country, took place on Monday last at Manchester.

The place appointed for the meeting was a large vacant piece of ground on the north side of St. Peter's Church, which is well known in Manchester by the name of St. Peter's-place. At half-past ten o'clock about 250 idle individuals might be collected within it. About half-past eleven the first body of Reformers arrived on the ground, bearing two banners, each of which was surmounted by a cap of liberty. The first bore the inscription of "Annual Parliaments, and Universal Suffrage;" on the reverse, "No Corn Laws." The other bore the same inscription, with the addition of "Vote by Ballot." After these flags had been paraded for some time, a post was assigned to the bearers

From the *Examiner* of 22 August 1819

Doubtless Shelley meant the herbivorous lions of *Queen Mab*; but to Leigh Hunt this looked like inflammatory stuff, and he prudently laid it, and all the political poems, aside, including the powerful *Sonnet to England in 1819*.

Two other political works of the autumn of 1819 must be mentioned. One was an open letter to the *Examiner* on the trial of Richard Carlile for blasphemous libel. Carlile was a disciple of Thomas Paine and was sentenced to three years' imprisonment and a huge fine for publishing his works; Shelley wrote at length in his defence, but Hunt did not publish the letter. The other work was *Peter Bell the Third*. Wordsworth's *Peter Bell* had already been mocked by Keats's friend Reynolds; Shelley had him taken up by the devil, and shown the world – 'Hell is a city much like London' begins the finest section. Peter is intended partly as Wordsworth ('a kind of moral eunuch'), although in one section his savaging by the reviewers parallels Shelley's experience; this was the time he read an attack on his private life in the *Quarterly Review*. Mary Shelley truthfully, and rather nervously, insisted on Shelley's admiration for Wordsworth's poetry in her edition; but *Peter Bell* is undoubtedly an attack on his degeneracy in becoming a poet of the Establishment, and thereby a dull one – 'Dull – beyond all conception – dull'. This too remained unpublished in Shelley's lifetime: one of his wittiest, most Byronic works.

In October the Shelleys moved to Florence, considered the safest place for the delivery of Mary's baby. Claire's brother left and a few days later, on 12 November, Percy Florence ('small but pretty') made an untroubled arrival at their lodgings in the Palazzo Marini, Via Valfonda. Shelley haunted the 'Florence gallery' (the Uffizi); he was also writing at a great rate. A plaque on a modern block of flats near the station records today that it stands on the site of the wood where he saw the leaves blowing, 'Yellow, and pale, and black, and hectic red' and was inspired to ask for the wind's destroying and preserving strength in his poetry. The *Ode to the West Wind* has been memorized by a million schoolchildren; even when they have not puzzled out its meaning they must have felt the excitement of its imagery of clouds and sea and branches, and the driving force of the *terza rima*.

In Florence too he wrote the final act of *Prometheus Unbound*, which he considered his best work. It is a play, but not for performance; a lyrical drama modelled on Aeschylus but bringing language closer to the condition of music than any Greek did. Commentators worry at the precise symbolism of Demogorgon (primal urge? revolutionary voice of the people?), Asia and the Moon; but perhaps *Prometheus* is best taken as a prolonged inner meditation on the theme

> The good want power, but to weep barren tears.
> The powerful goodness want: worse need for them.
> The wise want love; and those who love want wisdom;
> And all best things are thus confused to ill.

– interspersed with lyrics, now terrifying and now hopeful, given to Furies and Spirits who can also be seen as states of mind. Returning

Houses on the Lung'Arno, Pisa; l'Albergo di Tre Donzelle, where Shelley's party stayed briefly, is in the centre

to the question asked in *Mont Blanc* about the relation between power and evil in the universe, Shelley sends Asia, the bride of Prometheus, to visit the oracle Demogorgon in his cave and question him. Who made the good in the universe? she asks. To this he answers, God. She then asks who made terror, crime, pain and hell, to which Demogorgon replies cryptically, 'He reigns'. Pressed by Asia, he admits that Jupiter is enslaved to a master, but when Asia asks the name of this master, he answers 'the deep truth is imageless'. Asia agrees that she knows this in her heart already and that 'of such truths / Each to itself must be the oracle'.

The hero who embodies the whole of human suffering and nobility, the tyrant who is overthrown by fate (or sleight of hand, or a volcanic eruption) remain nebulous. Unless *Prometheus* is read as a meditation, the criticism most often levelled at Shelley's poetry, that it is diffuse and imprecise, with a 'weak grasp upon the actual', takes hold damagingly: some will say, even when it is. It was, however, accepted for publication by Ollier, who perhaps appreciated that its parallels were with the prophetic books of the Bible rather than with anything more recent and dangerous.

In December a young English girl, Sophia Stacey, the ward of one of Shelley's uncles, arrived in Florence with her chaperone, and Shelley and Claire spent a good deal of time taking them round the galleries and generally amusing them. The weather was unusually cold, and Mary spent most of her time in bed, with a work-table at hand as well as the thriving baby. Shelley was charmed by Sophia, and she by him: 'I fear thy kisses, gentle maiden,' is thought to have been addressed to her. At the end of the year she departed for Rome.

All through January it continued freezing, with snow on the ground. Shelley blamed Florence for making the pains in his side worse, and as soon as a thaw came he carried Mary, Claire and Percy off to Pisa by boat. They settled in rooms in a large house on the Arno, Casa Frassi. Milly had left them in Florence, and all their servants were now Italian.

The new delight of Pisa was the friendship of the Mason family, which Shelley had met briefly on his way through the city the previous September. 'Mrs Mason' was in fact Lady Mountcashel; both her father and her husband were Irish peers, but she had abandoned them and her many legitimate children in favour of George Tighe, to whom she bore two daughters. They lived a life of discreet happiness in Italy, and she busied herself with writing books on child care. She had known Godwin for many years, through her passionate interest in Irish politics; and she had another even stronger link with the Shelleys. As a girl she had been the favourite pupil of Mary's mother, in the 1780s when Mary Wollstonecraft worked as a governess in Ireland. Now, rather curiously, she became far more warmly interested in Claire than in Mary. In February relations between Mary and Claire were not at their best. 'A bad wife is like Winter in a house', wrote Claire sententiously in her journal. Meanwhile, Shelley was writing to the Gisbornes about his efforts to raise extra money, presumably for Elena in Naples; all this was kept secret from Mary, and the Gisbornes were asked to write to Shelley privately under the alias 'Mr Jones'.

He had further preoccupations; in March *The Cenci* was published in England and he was anxious that it should be staged. It was not. And news of the Cato Street conspiracy, in which five conspirators who had planned to assassinate Lord Liverpool and his ministers were caught and executed, gave him no cause for joy in either the attempt or the punishment. His general gloom found expression in his poem *The Sensitive Plant*, which depicted in rather eerie detail the decay and destruction of a once blooming garden, and the death of the sensitive plant itself.

In April Shelley was telling Hunt that they saw no one but the Masons, and that they planned to move to Bagni di Lucca in June; adding that he would like to go to Spain, where a successful revolution had taken place. To Medwin he described himself as an invalid who saw nobody, and to Hogg, whom he also pressed to join him, he complained of having been deprived of his company by 'the unfortunate and almost inexplicable complexity of my situation'. His thoughts turned much to English friends; he even asked Hogg if he had news of the Boinvilles, and lamented to Peacock 'we know little of England here'. The year before, he had asked Ollier twice to make sure of sending anything he published of his to Keats. In May 1820 he lauded Keats to Ollier as a potential great poet, and in July, hearing of his illness, he wrote directly to him inviting him to Pisa as his guest, praising his *Endymion*, which he had just re-read, and telling him to expect copies of *The Cenci* and *Prometheus*. Keats's reply came with courteous speed, suggesting that he might indeed visit the Shelleys unless prevented by a 'circumstance I have very much at heart to prophesy' (i.e. his death). He had only six months to live, and wrote letters with difficulty; but his acutely intelligent criticism of Shelley's poetry, of which he never knew the best, is expressed with perfect sympathy and tact:

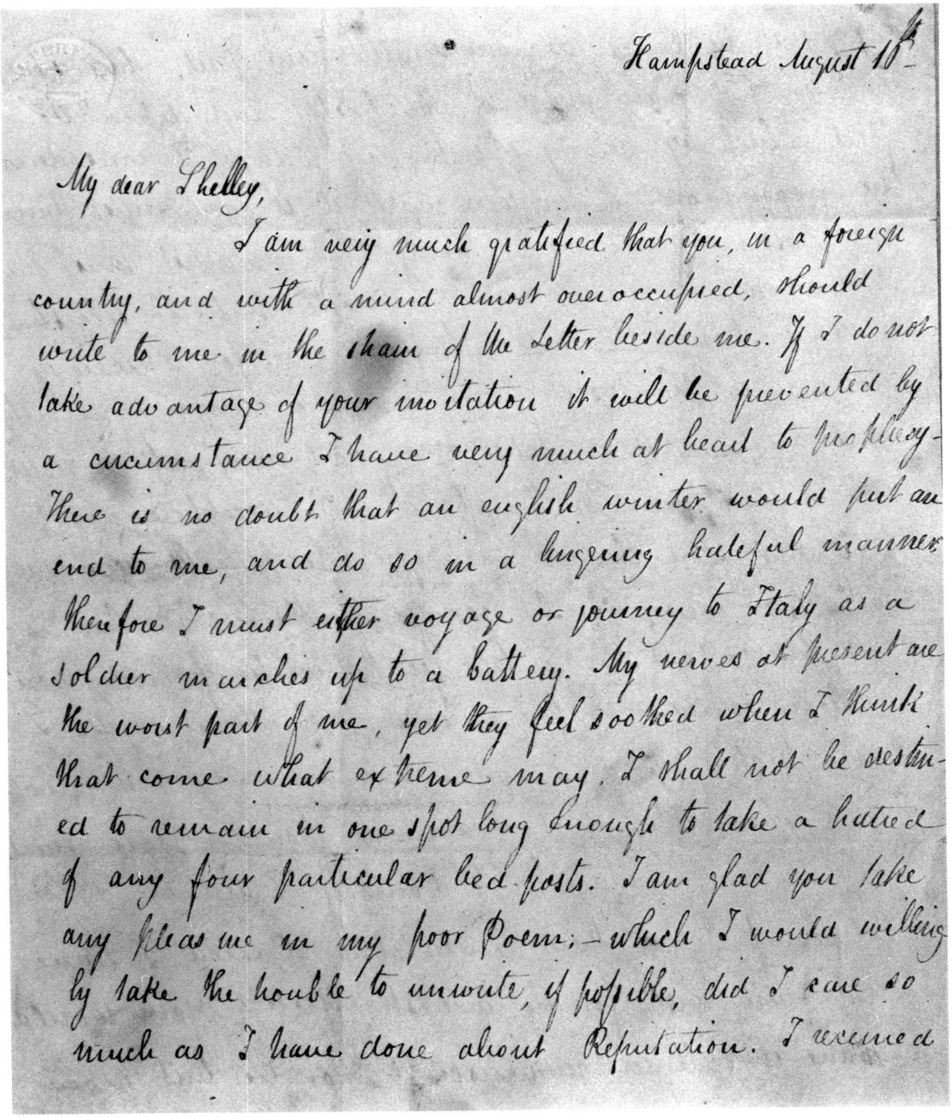

Hampstead August 16

My dear Shelley,

I am very much gratified that you, in a foreign country, and with a mind almost over occupied, should write to me in the strain of the Letter beside me. If I do not take advantage of your invitation it will be prevented by a circumstance I have very much at heart to prophesy. There is no doubt that an english winter would put an end to me, and do so in a lingering hateful manner. Therefore I must either voyage or journey to Italy as a soldier marches up to a battery. My nerves at present are the worst part of me, yet they feel soothed when I think that come what extreme may, I shall not be destined to remain in one spot long enough to take a hatred of any four particular bed-posts. I am glad you take any pleasure in my poor Poem; — which I would willingly take the trouble to unwrite, if possible, did I care so much as I have done about Reputation. I received

I received a copy of the Cenci, as from yourself, from Hunt. There is only one part of it I am judge of – the poetry and dramatic effect which by many spirits nowadays is considered the Mammon. A modern work, it is said, must have a purpose, which may be the God. An artist must serve Mammon; he must have 'self-concentration' – selfishness, perhaps. You, I am sure, will forgive me for sincerely remarking that you might curb your magnanimity, and be more of an artist, and load every rift of your subject with ore. The thought of such discipline must fall like cold chains upon you, who perhaps never sat with your wings furled for six months together.

Keats's letter to Shelley, August 1820

Shelley had been busy with more prose, his *Philosophical View of Reform*, a long essay partly historical and partly descriptive of the present state of England with its sinister new merchant aristocracy ('pelting wretches'): 'the power which has increased . . . is the power of the rich. . . . Monarchy is only the string which ties the robber's bundle.' He returned to his old themes of the misery of the poor, the unequal distribution of wealth, wrong system of taxation and defectiveness of the government. Every enlightened and honourable person, he urged, should excite the people to 'temperate but irresistible vindication of their rights':

> the last resort of resistance is undoubtedly insurrection. – The right of insurrection is derived from the employment of armed forces to counteract the will of the nation.

Of course no publisher could print this. It was not printed, in fact, until 1920. Shelley felt himself still a pariah.

As though biting on an aching tooth, he now decided to write to Southey, suspecting his hand in the hostile remarks of the *Quarterly*. Through the summer months the two poets exchanged letters of rebuke, Southey attacking Shelley directly for his private life and blaming him for Harriet's death, Shelley responding with anguished self-righteousness. His anguish was sharpened because in July he had news of the death of Elena; and at the same time Paolo Foggi began to blackmail him over her parentage. In order to see the lawyer who advised him, Shelley went with Mary and Claire to the Gisbornes' house, Casa Ricci, at Leghorn. The Gisbornes themselves were away in London; and here Shelley's quicksilver nature let him write one of his most pleasant poems, the *Letter to Maria Gisborne*, an exercise in heroic couplets which moved from a description of his surroundings in Italy to a discussion of what the Gisbornes were doing in London. He imagines them seeing Godwin, or rather

> That which was Godwin, – greater none than he
> Though fallen – and fallen on evil times – to stand
> Among the spirits of our age and land,
> Before the dread tribunal of *to come*
> The foremost, – while Rebuke cowers pale and dumb.

It must be set to Shelley's credit that he wrote this at the same time as he found himself forced to send a letter of severe rebuke to Godwin for his unceasing monetary claims; Shelley said he had given him between £4,000 and £5,000 in the last few years, had debts of his own and commitments unknown even to Mary. The letter also gives a picture of his coming reunion in Italy with the Gisbornes:

> Though we eat little flesh and drink no wine,
> Yet let's be merry: we'll have tea and toast;
> Custards for supper, and an endless host
> Of syllabubs and jellies and mince-pies,
> And other such lady-like luxuries, –
> Feasting on which we will philosophize!
> And we'll have fires out of the Grand Duke's wood,
> To thaw the six weeks' winter in our blood.

Rooted in what he knows, has seen and felt for himself, in something precise, the verse sparkles and lives.

Bagni di San Giuliano, on the
canal, near Pisa

In August Shelley took Mary, Claire and Percy to Bagni di Pisa (or
Bagni di San Giuliano: the two names refer to the same place). The
house, Casa Prinni, backed on to a canal joining the rivers Arno and
Serchio, which he enjoyed exploring. From there they made an
expedition to Lucca, where Mary's new novel *Castruccio* was set;
Shelley went on alone to climb Monte San Pellegrino, coming back
with *The Witch of Atlas* in his head; he completed it in three days. The
witch is an impish, beautiful dream creature, daughter of the Sun and
'one of the Atlantides', who travels about in a magic boat guided by a
hermaphrodite of her own creation, playing tricks with the natural
world (like Ariel) and meddling in human dreams (like Shakespeare's
Mab). It is an almost defiantly frolicsome work, as though Shelley
were showing off his mythmaking and technical ease; the same effect
is felt in *The Cloud* and *To a Skylark*, dazzling exercises that do not
invite too many re-readings.

Claire was due to leave for Leghorn, for some sea bathing. Before she went, news came of a revolution in Naples, duly noted in her diary:

> the people assembled round the palace demanding a Constitution; the King ordered his troops to fire and disperse the crowd; they refused, and he has now promised a Constitution. . . . This is glorious, and is produced by the Revolution in Spain.

Shelley greeted the good news with an *Ode to Naples*. Unfortunately neither this nor the *Ode to Liberty* which had greeted the news from Spain shows him entirely comfortable with his material; the mixture of historical précis with invocations to Pity, Indignation, Chaos, Oppression, etc., however melodious, grows oppressive. The exception is the last stanza of *Liberty*, with its terrible, prophetic image:

> Then, as a wild swan, when sublimely winging
> Its path athwart the thunder-smoke of dawn,
> Sinks headlong through the aëreal golden light
> On the heavy-sounding plain,
> When the bolt has pierced its brain;
> As summer clouds dissolve, unburthened of their rain;
> As a far taper fades with fading night,
> As a brief insect dies with dying day, –
> My song, its pinions disarrayed of might,
> Drooped; o'er it closed the echoes far away
> Of the great voice which did its flight sustain,
> As waves which lately paved his watery way
> Hiss round a drowner's head in their tempestuous play.

Another composition of this summer, *Swellfoot the Tyrant*, a satirical pantomime on the manner in which George IV was conducting his marital disagreements with Queen Caroline, suggests that Shelley saw and entered into the spirit of the brutal political cartoons that kept England vulgarly agog. His chorus of pigs and other animal characters were all found among them, and rise to no very high level of wit. But during the same months he continued to write short lyrics of surpassing splendour, notably *The Question*, a wild flower catalogue of Elizabethan exuberance which ends on a wholly nineteenth-century note of sudden, dramatic desolation; and *The Two Spirits*, discussed later in these pages.

Now distractions arrived one after another. Claire was persuaded, largely by Mrs Mason, to try a formal separation from the Shelleys. She was reluctant and he unhappy, but in October he took her to Florence and left her as half paying guest, half companion to the daughters of Dr Bojti, court physician to the Grand Duke Ferdinand. Shelley's letters to her are not exactly love-letters, but their phrasing – 'my best girl', 'my own Clare', 'my dearest Clare', 'be careful to tear this letter to pieces' – implies a private intimacy and mutually acknowledged dependence; and he divulged to her his wish to embark on a trip to Greece and the East, suggesting she might be one of the party, and warning her not to tell Mary.

After depositing Claire, Shelley met his cousin Tom Medwin, who had journeyed from Geneva at his suggestion. The two had not seen

Edward Ellerker Williams
(1793–1822): a self-portrait,
washed ashore in the wreckage of
the *Ariel*

one another for seven years but Medwin had no difficulty in recognizing the tall, emaciated, stooping figure, now with grey streaks in his hair. They reached Bagni just in time for a flood caused by the torrential autumn rains, and had to move back to Pisa at once, where they settled in the Palazzo Galetti. Medwin promptly fell ill; Shelley nursed him tenderly, and Medwin used his inactivity to read his cousin's works, with growing admiration. His friendliness was the more welcome in the absence of Claire and because of a temporary rift which had arisen between the Shelleys and the Gisbornes since their return from London.

Claire returned for a while in November; and now the Shelleys began to find a whole circle of new acquaintances: John Taaffe, an Irish expatriate with a literary turn, whom they regarded as a bore, but an amiable one; and an exiled Greek prince, Alexander Mavrocordato, who became Mary's admirer. An Italian friend was the unorthodox and amusing university teacher, Francesco Pacchiani; through him first Claire and then the Shelleys were introduced to the daughter of the governor of Pisa, Teresa Emilia Viviani, who was living in a convent much against her will while her father and stepmother arranged her marriage. She was very young, and enchanted to have English friends interested in her fate; Shelley was captivated by her. She showed him her essay *Il vero amore*, called him brother, sympathized with his ill-health. Mary and Claire were her sisters, although Mary's *freddezza* troubled her. To Shelley Emilia appeared flawless.

In January 1821 Medwin's friends the Williamses arrived in Pisa; they were gradually to take a central position in Shelley's life. Edward Williams was then in his mid-twenties; born in India, he had been

Jane Williams painted by George Clint

sent back to England, and indeed Eton, for two years, at the same time as Shelley. Williams left, still a child, to become a midshipman, and later an officer in the army of the East India Company. In India he met Jane, who had been taken there by her brother, married unhappily and separated almost at once from her husband. Unable to marry, they left the East together and lived on his half-pay, passing their time in travel and mildly cultural activities; she was musical, he wrote and drew a little.

Williams soon became Shelley's favourite companion; and Jane, whom he characterized to Claire as 'an extremely pretty & gentle woman – apparently not *very* clever' in first meeting her, grew in his affections, not least because he found her warm-hearted. He envied the close attachment between the Williamses and contrasted it with the now established chill of his own domesticity.

As the year went on he needed some renewal in his life. In February Medwin departed, and Keats died in Rome, although the news did not reach Pisa for two months. In July the Gisbornes were to leave for

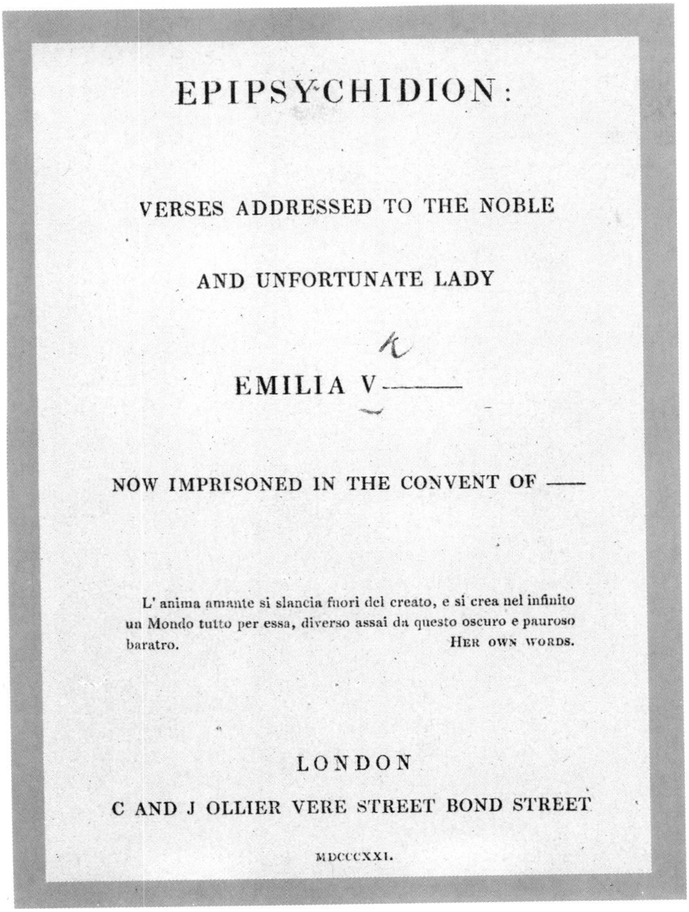

EPIPSYCHIDION:

VERSES ADDRESSED TO THE NOBLE

AND UNFORTUNATE LADY

EMILIA V——

NOW IMPRISONED IN THE CONVENT OF ——

L' anima amante si slancia fuori del creato, e si crea nel infinito un Mondo tutto per essa, diverso assai da questo oscuro e pauroso baratro. HER OWN WORDS.

LONDON

C AND J OLLIER VERE STREET BOND STREET

MDCCCXXI.

The title-page of Shelley's *Epipsychidion*: 'it is a production of a portion of me already dead . . . and I make its author a secret, to avoid the malignity of those who turn sweet food into poison.' (Shelley to Ollier)

England again; Claire was away in Florence or Leghorn most of the year, Mary had her own writing and the care of Percy, although she loyally continued to copy for Shelley; and Emilia Viviani's light as Platonic ideal was to flicker and go out.

Meanwhile, she blazed as few poets' mistresses have ever blazed. Inspired by his feeling for her, and by reading the *Vita nuova*, in which Dante gave an idealized account of his love, Shelley produced a six-hundred-line poem in couplets, in which he explained his view of love, proceeded to a partly cryptic and partly all-too-clear autobiographical section, and culminated in a passionate invitation to Emilia to embark with him for – in effect – Cytherea. The *Epipsychidion* (Shelley's coinage, meaning roughly 'little external soul') stands among his most extraordinary and successful poems; it has never failed to attract readers for its unmistakable and delicious eroticism, its easy flowing pace and brilliant images, its hints of self-revelation and, not least, its straightforward attack on marriage and defence of free love:

> I never was attached to that great sect,
> Whose doctrine is, that each one should select
> Out of the crowd a mistress or a friend,
> And all the rest, though fair and wise, commend
> To cold oblivion, though it is in the code
> Of modern morals, and the beaten road
> Which those poor slaves with weary footsteps tread,
> Who travel to their home among the dead
> By the broad highway of the world, and so
> With one chained friend, perhaps a jealous foe,
> The dreariest and the longest journey go.

The puzzle of the *Epipsychidion* is that it tries simultaneously to celebrate free love and courtly, ideal love. The difficulty, or impossibility, of squaring the two – of reconciling total commitment with diverse affectionate and erotic impulses – so painfully present in Shelley's life, was here made somehow into the germ and driving force of the poem and is undoubtedly a reason for its appeal. 'Spouse', 'sister', 'angel', 'dream', he calls Emilia, though all the imagery of the poem spells out the sexual longing. The fantasy of a guiltless eroticism tied to a better social system, in which no one is shackled but each freely chooses perfect happiness, speaks persuasively to all who suffer and struggle in that particular web:

> We two will rise, and sit, and walk together,
> Under the roof of blue Ionian weather,
> And wander in the meadows, or ascend
> The mossy mountains, where the blue heavens bend
> With lightest winds, to touch their paramour;
> Or linger, where the pebble-paven shore,
> Under the quick, faint kisses of the sea
> Trembles and sparkles as with ecstasy, –
> Possessing and possessed by all that is
> Within that calm circumference of bliss,
> And by each other, till to love and live
> Be one . . .

Almost as soon as Shelley had sent the poem off to Ollier, with an elaborate introductory note explaining that the author was dead and instructions to publish anonymously, he regretted it, and later tried to suppress the edition. He partly explained his change of heart to Gisborne:

> I think one is always in love with something or other; the error, and I confess it is not easy for spirits encased in flesh and blood to avoid it, consists in seeking in mortal image the likeness of what is perhaps eternal.

The pain caused to Mary, whose coldness is insisted on in the autobiographical part of the poem (where Claire appears as a 'fierce comet'), was a cruel infliction, and the *Epipsychidion* is one of the few poems she did not annotate in her edition.

The rest of February and March were devoted to what became his best-known prose work, *A Defence of Poetry*; it was inspired by a jocular essay of Peacock, who asserted that poetry was no longer a fit occupation for intelligent beings. In his reply Shelley based his argument on an extension of the meaning of the word poetry to cover virtually the whole field of the moral, as opposed to the scientific and practical imagination, ending with the claim that poets are the unacknowledged legislators of the world. If indeed poetry stands for the power of the human imagination to change mankind, Shelley's claim is justified. His further idealization of poets as the 'wisest, happiest and best' of men, characterized by 'spotless virtue' and 'consummate prudence' looks a little less bizarre if they are being considered purely in their aspect of spiritual guides to the dull mass of humanity. Shelley used sections of his *Philosophical View of Reform* in the *Defence*, notably its account of the development of civilization, and cannibalized a good many passages from other writings of his own; the brilliant apologia for Milton's Satan, for instance, from *On Devils*. The *Defence* was intended as part of a longer work, never composed; it was not published in his lifetime. Mary issued it in 1840 and it became a classic text, perhaps because it expresses views people feel poets ought to hold, as well as for its fine, enthusiastic language.

In his role as unacknowledged legislator, Shelley was able to rejoice on 1 April, when Prince Mavrocordato brought jubilant news that the Greeks had risen against their Turkish oppressors. The Prince prepared to depart to join in the fight; but Shelley was soon telling Medwin he felt disinclined to continue with his own project of visiting Greece because the Greeks were now massacring the Turks.

A few weeks later Shelley went with Williams and Reveley to Leghorn to buy a small boat for use on the rivers and canals; on the way back they had an accident in the dark and Shelley was pulled half-drowned from the canal. He laughed it off, seeing it as a good omen. In May he and Mary moved to Bagni again, the Williamses going to nearby Pugnano, and the summer developed its routine. Shelley walked often into Pisa, visiting the Masons and Emilia. Taaffe called assiduously. Mavrocordato made his preparations to leave, the Gisbornes were packing and Claire spent most of her summer at Leghorn. From England the Hunts wrote of their financial troubles; and Shelley was amused to hear of a pirated publication of *Queen Mab* – he had refused Richard Carlile permission to reprint it in 1819. It led to the publisher being sentenced to four months' imprisonment in spite of his plea that he had no ideological interest in the work. During the next twenty years fourteen editions appeared, and *Queen Mab* became essential reading for all English radicals.

News of the death of Keats reached Shelley in May; he had been trying to reach him through Medwin, who had gone to Rome, weeks after Keats had been laid in the Protestant cemetery. Convinced that he had been hounded to death by the reviewers, Shelley set to writing his great elegy, *Adonais*. In the introductory notes to *Epipsychidion* he had already described his own death; his identification with Keats, driven to an early grave by persecution and illness, was obvious and, as no critic has failed to point out, *Adonais* is as much a lament for himself as for the younger poet: 'the sepulchre of a humanist and heroic quest', as Harold Bloom has said. Formal in stanza and overall

Prince Alexander Mavrocordato, a Greek leader in exile. 'We are surrounded here in Pisa by revolutionary volcanoes', wrote Shelley

structure, highly wrought in diction, it achieves, after a somewhat strained and long-drawn-out opening section, a wonderful rolling momentum and some phrases of plangent grief:

> Why linger, why turn back, why shrink, my Heart?
> Thy hopes are gone before: from all things here
> They have departed; thou shouldst now depart!
> A light is passed from the revolving year,
> And man, and woman; and what still is dear
> Attracts to crush, repels to make thee wither.
> The soft sky smiles, – the low wind whispers near:
> 'Tis Adonais calls! oh, hasten thither,
> No more let Life divide what Death can join together.

A copy of *Adonais* was sent to Byron in Ravenna: 'I send you – as Diomed gave Glaucus his brazen arms for those of gold – some verses I wrote on the death of Keats', says Shelley modestly. Since May the two survivors had been hoping to meet and renew their friendly conversations; Shelley had also to discuss Claire's wish to see Allegra again. At the beginning of August he set off. He did not go directly, but went first to Leghorn where Claire was, arriving late on the evening of the 3rd. The next day was his 29th birthday. This was Claire's journal entry:

> Saturday August 4th. S's Birthday 29 yrs. Rise at five – Row in the Harbour with S – Then call upon the Countess Tolomei. Then we sail out into the sea. A very fine warm day. the white sails of ships upon the horizon looked like doves stooping over the water. Dine at the Giardinetto. S – goes at two.

As soon as he arrived in Ravenna Byron showed him a letter, received nearly a year before, from their old friend Hoppner, the Venetian consul-general. It contained the assertion that Shelley and Claire had had a child in Naples and there abandoned it in the Foundling Hospital; and that they had previously tried to procure an abortion, and consistently deceived and abused Mary. The information came from Elise and was believed by the Hoppners; Byron thought the story credible but considered Elise an unreliable witness, as she clearly was. Shelley's immediate reaction to the letter was to write to Mary asking her to deny the story 'which you only can effectually rebut', and this she did in the most impassioned terms, asserting that her marriage was 'ever undisturbed'. Neither mentioned Elena, it seems, and if Claire was informed, no record remains of it. Perhaps Shelley's talks with Byron were less discreet than his letters to Mary; at all events Byron kept Mary's letter and did not show it to the Hoppners. The following spring Elise visited Claire in Florence and threw her into a state of deep disturbance, culminating in her asking Mary to tell *her*, Claire, what to tell Elise to write to the Hoppners by way of denial. If Elena was Claire's child, the one thing that neither Mary, nor Byron, nor the Hoppners, nor Elise, nor anyone else (except perhaps Peacock, had he been at hand) could understand was that Shelley might genuinely love both Mary and Claire, as he clearly did. If he could not explain this, there was little point in explaining anything else.

Countess Teresa Guiccioli: 'a very pretty sentimental, innocent, superficial Italian, who has sacrificed an immense fortune to live for Lord Byron; and who, if I know anything of my friend, of her, or of human nature will hereafter have plenty of leisure and opportunity to repent of her rashness.' (Shelley to John Gisborne)

Byron managed things more brutally, and more easily. In Ravenna Shelley met his mistress, Countess Teresa Guiccioli, now separated from her husband. He thought her a soothing influence on Byron, and she was charmed by Shelley, and gave an interesting account of him later:

It was said that in his adolescence he was good-looking – but now he was no longer so. His features were delicate but not regular – except for his mouth which however was not good when he laughed, and was a little spoiled by his teeth, the shape of which was not in keeping with his refinement. . . . He was also extraordinary in his garb, for he normally wore a jacket like a young college boy's, never any gloves nor polish on his boots – and yet among a thousand he would always have seemed the most finished of gentlemans [*sic*]. His voice was shrill – even strident, and nevertheless it was modulated by the drift of his thoughts with a grace, a gentleness, a delicacy that went to the heart. . . . Perhaps never did anyone ever see a man so deficient in beauty who still could produce an impression of it. . . . It was the fire, the enthusiasm, of his Intelligence that transformed his features.

Believed to be a drawing of
Shelley by Edward Williams

In one way Byron cheered Shelley, by his genuine friendliness and by
imposing a completely alien daily routine, consisting of rising in the
middle of the day, talking till six, riding, and sitting up all night. Yet
he confessed, to Peacock, his despondency at his own failure as a
poet, in contrast to Byron's fame:

> I write nothing, and probably shall write no more. It offends me to see my
> name classed among those who have no name. If I cannot be something
> better, I had rather be nothing . . .

To Mary also he wrote,

> I would retire with you and our child to a solitary island in the sea, would
> build a boat, and shut upon my retreat the floodgates of the world. I would
> read no reviews, and talk with no authors. If I dared trust my imagination
> it would tell me that there were two or three chosen companions besides
> yourself whom I should desire. But to this I would not listen – where two
> or three are gathered together the devil is among them. And good far more
> than evil impulses – love far more than hatred, has been to me, except as
> you have been its object, the source of all sort of mischief.

Against this wounded cry must be set the knowledge that Shelley was welcoming Byron's project to come to Pisa, ready to change his own plan of wintering in Florence to be with him, and was very shortly to find the company of the Williamses utterly indispensable.

While in Ravenna Shelley made two pilgrimages: one to the tomb of Dante, where he 'worshipped the sacred spot' and fancied a slight resemblance in the half-closed eye of the bust to his friend Pacchiani. The other, sadder visit was to the convent where Allegra was kept; he saw the nuns petting her, but observed too that she was subject to strict discipline. He took her a gold chain and some sweets; and although to him the worst part of her fate was the fact that she was being brought up to believe Catholic 'trash', he must have felt a pang at seeing her both fatherless and motherless. It was not what he had in mind when he brought her to Italy.

And now he returned to Pisa. In September Emilia was married and went off to live with her in-laws. The Shelleys were not invited to the wedding, and soon both were mentioning Emilia's name with hostility. (Emilia herself was unhappy in her marriage and died pathetically young.) Shelley settled down to write *Hellas*, fired by the events in Greece; it was another lyrical drama, dedicated to Mavrocordato, who was in fact the only Greek Shelley knew. But as he said, 'We are all Greeks. Our laws, our literature, our religion, our arts have their root in Greece.' The prefatory remarks went on to lament the lack of freedom in England and describe the rulers of Europe as 'ringleaders of the privileged gang of murderers and oppressors'. Ollier suppressed this paragraph but issued the drama itself, which consists of dialogue between Mahmud, a Turkish ruler, the Wandering Jew Ahasuerus and various messengers, phantoms and voices without, interspersed with choruses spoken by captive Greek women. *Hellas*, which Shelley himself called 'a mere improvise', is rarely read except for its celebrated choruses; too much of it is fuzzy and grandiose. Two other dramas were embarked on, as though he were casting about uncertainly, one an entertainment for his friends, involving an Indian enchantress and a pirate, and another, more serious, work on Charles I. What there is of this shows that Shelley intended a carefully balanced account of the English revolution; and the influence of Shakespeare is again strongly felt. The best thing is the song of the jester, Archy, as bleakly perfect as anything in English poetry, and not without echoes of Shelley's 1816 poem on Harriet's death:

> A widow bird sate mourning for her love
>   Upon a wintry bough;
> The frozen wind crept on above,
>   The freezing stream below.
>
> There was no leaf upon the forest bare,
>   No flower upon the ground,
> And little motion in the air
>   Except the mill-wheel's sound.

Tre Palazzi di Chiesa: the Shelleys and the Williamses each took a floor in this Pisan palace

Detail from Joseph Severn's portrait of Trelawny (1792–1881): he was '6 feet high, with raven black hair which curls thickly and shortly, like a Moor's . . . and a smile which expresses good nature and kind heartedness', wrote Mary

By November Shelley had settled himself and Mary on the top floor of a Pisan palazzo on the Arno, with, for the first time in Italy, their own furniture. The Williamses were on the floor below and Byron opposite. Claire left for Florence as Byron arrived with the Countess and her brother, Count Gamba. Although Byron had Teresa with him, he imposed a routine of all-male dinners and sporting activities. He was the better rider, Shelley the better shot despite his short sight; and with Williams they agreed on a passion for boating. They decided, 'without asking our consent, or having our concurrence', said Mary, to have boats built and spend the summer of 1822 on the Bay of Lerici, where they could sail uninterruptedly. The arrival of a friend of Williams and Medwin, Edward Trelawny, acted as a spur to this project. Trelawny had spent an adventurous life at sea. Mary found him delightful company but was uncertain as to his moral qualities, she told Mrs Gisborne. His fame rests entirely on the fact that he knew Shelley for a few months, Byron for a little longer and wrote one of the most vivid, if not always reliable, accounts of them.

Palazzo Lanfranchi on the Arno at Pisa, where Byron settled in 1821 at Shelley's invitation

The early months of 1822 saw Shelley busy trying to raise more money for the Hunts, who had already received a great deal and whom he had sent for, with the idea that Leigh Hunt and Byron should run together a magazine to be called the *Liberal*. The Hunts had problems of their own: his brother was in prison and Marianne kept falling ill at the prospect of a long sea voyage with six children. But now Byron had furnished some rooms for their reception and put up £250 in addition to all the money Shelley had sent; and in May the Hunts finally set sail. Another problem in England was Ollier, who prevaricated over whether he would take on Mary's novel and whom Shelley was now referring to as an 'infinite thief'. Worse trouble was nearer at hand. Claire was quite reasonably concerned for Allegra's fate in the Bagnacavallo convent. Mr Mason took the trouble to visit the child and was upset enough by what he saw to urge that she should be recovered from Byron's care. Shelley, however, urged patience and inaction to Claire, mentioning Byron's 'jealousy of my regard for your interests' as one reason. 'It seems to me that you have no other resource but time and chance and change': bad advice, as it soon appeared. Claire was apparently thinking of trying to rescue Allegra by kidnapping her with the aid of a forged letter. Shelley's refusal to be party to this looks less impressive when one remembers the fake birth information concerning Elena, and his advice to Claire is of the kind he might well have taken more to heart himself:

> give up this idle pursuit after shadows, and temper yourself to the season, seek in the daily and affectionate intercourse of friends a respite from these perpetual and irritating projects. Live from day to day, attend to your health, cultivate literature and liberal ideas to a certain extent, and expect that from time and change which no exertion of your own can give you.

Perhaps Shelley was able to hand out this wisdom through contemplating the wreckage of his own perpetual pursuit of shadows and irritating projects. Peacock had dissuaded him from a plan to set off for India only lately; the Middle Eastern trip had fallen through; there had been small joy from Emilia. But a new shadow was dancing before him, that of Jane Williams, who seemed more bewitching from day to day. From now until the end of his life Shelley addressed a series of love poems to Jane in which he expressed his adoration of her and admiration of the happiness she and Williams enjoyed together. 'The serpent is shut out from Paradise', begins one; another describes Jane soothing Shelley's physical pains by magnetizing him. Like Claire she enchanted him with her music, and he sent for a guitar, which he gave her, calling himself Ariel to her Miranda. At the same time he wrote letters, one to Gisborne for instance, expressing his dissatisfaction with Mary, her lack of sympathy, her inability to accept many aspects of his personality and interests. He acknowledged that there might be something inherent in the domestic situation that made perfect sympathy impossible; but the Williamses seemed to suggest another possibility. Jane was bland enough to enjoy Shelley's devotion without feeling threatened by it and was perfectly agreeable to the plan that they should all summer together at Lerici.

The guitar Shelley gave to Jane Williams and (*opposite*) part of his fair copy of the poem that accompanied the gift

With a guitar. To Jane.

Ariel to Miranda;— Take
This slave of music for the sake
Of him who is the slave of thee;
And teach it all the harmony,
In which thou can'st, & only thou,
Make the delighted spirit glow,
Till joy denies itself again
And too intense is turned to pain;
For by permission & command
Of thine own prince Ferdinand
Poor Ariel sends this silent token
Of more than ever can be spoken;
Your guardian spirit Ariel, who
From life to life must still pursue
Your happiness, for thus alone
Can Ariel ever find his own;
From Prospero's enchanted cell,
As the mighty verses tell,

A putative sketch by Edward Williams of Shelley in which can be seen what he called his 'little turn up nose'. 'He was by no means what one would call a fine, handsome man; but ethereal-looking and gentle as he really was; with small features, very uncommon eyes, his hair in disorder. . . . There was a mixture of penetrating expression and childish simplicity together in his countenance.' (J. F. Newton's daughter in old age)

Before they left Pisa an incident of Anglo-Italian hostility took place. A drunken Italian dragoon, Sergeant-Major Masi, brushed past Taaffe as he was riding towards Pisa with Byron, Shelley, Trelawny, Count Gamba and a Captain Hay. Some of the party rode angrily in pursuit of Masi, who stopped at the gate and tried to have the guard intervene. A scuffle followed, in which Shelley was knocked off his horse, Hay cut on the face and, after further confusion, Masi was seriously wounded by one of Byron's servants. Everyone recovered and although rumours flew merrily about no serious trouble ensued; but Byron and the Gambas moved out of Pisa to Montenero, on the coast near Leghorn.

Claire now came over from Florence and accompanied the Williamses to La Spezia to try to find summer housing. When they returned without success Shelley had just heard the news of Allegra's death from typhus at Bagnacavallo on 19 April. Byron had known of her illness but thought it insufficiently serious to mention to anyone else. Shelley, fearing the possibility of a confrontation, did not tell Claire but hurried her straight back to La Spezia with Mary and Trelawny. He followed with the Williamses and they crammed

themselves into the only house available, Casa Magni. It was a bleak enough place, built on the very rocks of the seashore, uninhabitable at ground-floor level but with four rooms and a terrace on the first floor. Here, after a week in which Shelley failed to tell Claire, she guessed what had happened. With perfect justice she laid the blame upon Byron and regarded Shelley and Mary as to some extent participating in it. But her temperament had a self-balancing mechanism built into it; she was not a repiner or sulker and Shelley's fear that she might go mad was very far from the mark. She soon became quite calm and went back to Florence, on good enough terms with the Shelleys to agree to return to Casa Magni in the summer.

Mary was again pregnant, the baby expected in December; she was in low spirits and bad temper, hating the cramped and difficult domestic arrangements at Casa Magni, where the servants slept out, the nearest hamlet at San Terenzo was useless for supplies and the local fishermen and their wives seemed like savages. Shelley's increasing adoration of Jane can hardly have improved her mood. News of her father's grotesque money troubles continued to filter through to her in spite of Shelley's wish to protect her from this at least.

Casa Magni, near San Terenzo, La Spezia: 'the sea came up to the door, a steep hill sheltered it behind. . . . Had we been wrecked on an island in the South Seas, we could scarcely have felt ourselves farther from civilization and comfort.' (Mary Shelley)

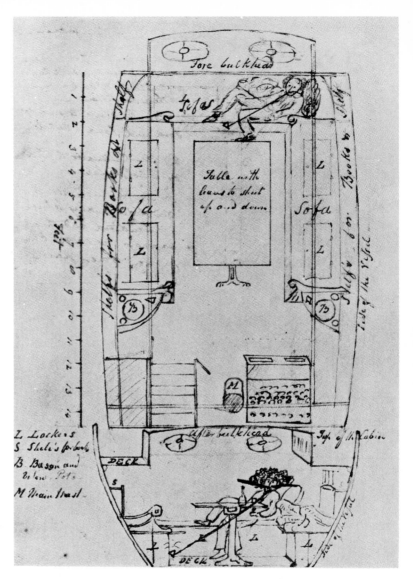

'Ours was to be an open boat, on a model taken from one of the royal dockyards. I have since heard that there was a defect in this model, and that it was never seaworthy.' (Mary Shelley) Edward Williams's sketch plan of the cabin of the *Don Juan* (or *Ariel*) and (*opposite*) his drawing of both it and Byron's *Bolivar*

In May the specially built boat arrived, to the delight of Shelley and Williams. Trelawny had gone off to sail with Byron in his *Bolivar*, and was responsible for naming the smaller boat the *Don Juan*, which annoyed Shelley, who had decided to call it the *Ariel*. They cut the sail to remove the offending name and began their sailing at once, assisted by a young English sailor, Charles Vivian, one of those who had brought her over from Genoa where she was built by Captain Daniel Roberts, a friend of Trelawny. He suggested that a Genoese sailor would be a useful addition to the crew – the boat was fast and rode high, and Shelley was vague in his seamanship – but Williams would have none of it.

In June Claire arrived at Casa Magni again, apparently in good spirits. During the following week Mary became ill and suffered a miscarriage which threatened her life through loss of blood. Shelley's early interest in anatomy stood him in good stead; ice was sent for and he mady Mary sit in it. Presumably it stopped further haemorrhage; when the doctor arrived he said Shelley had done the right thing. Mary recovered but remained acutely depressed. He insisted that everything was delightful at Casa Magni, although he suffered from nightmares and hallucinations. The first was of a naked child, like Allegra, rising out of the sea and clapping its hands. The second was an encounter with his own *Doppelgänger* on the terrace, who asked him 'How long do you mean to be content?' The third, and most appalling, was a double vision, first of the Williamses coming into his room, bloody and mangled, to warn him that the house was coming down; and when he rushed into Mary's room to tell her, he saw himself strangling her. About this time he wrote to Trelawny asking if he could provide him with a lethal dose of prussic acid, not for immediate use but because 'it would be a comfort to me to hold in my possession that golden key to the chamber of perpetual rest'. The fluctuations of his mood were intense; at times he was claiming to be supremely happy, at any rate out on the water in the summer moonlight, Jane beside him playing her guitar:

> if the past and the future could be obliterated, the present would content me so well that I could say with Faust to the passing moment, 'Remain, thou art so beautiful'.

Yet *The Triumph of Life*, a poem in sharp, springy *terza rima*, unfinished at his death, suggests a deep and terrible disillusionment with the world. Its image of the huge chariot of life travelling on like a juggernaut, surrounded by a boiling, insect-like crowd of humanity feverishly pursuing pleasure and ambition before being extinguished, is the most hideous he imagined.

Hunt and his family arrived in Genoa and prepared to continue their journey to Leghorn. Shelley was eager to go to meet his old friend and on 1 July he set off in the *Don Juan*, which Captain Roberts had been refitting. Roberts, Vivian and Williams sailed with Shelley, and they reached Leghorn in seven hours, sleeping that night still aboard, on cushions from the *Bolivar*. In the morning the quarantine officers allowed them ashore and the reunion took place in Byron's presence. Shelley was in high spirits, laughing, and looking well. He set off for Pisa with Hunt and remained there five days, occupied in smoothing relations between Hunt and Byron, already exasperated by the troop of Hunt children. Both men wanted Shelley to stay longer, but Williams was anxious to return and Shelley had wife, child, Claire and Jane each in a different way demanding his return. On 7 July he called on the Masons and set off for Leghorn again. The weather looked unsettled; Trelawny's intention of sailing alongside them in the *Bolivar* was prevented by port formalities. Eleven months earlier Shelley had sailed in the bay with Claire on his twenty-ninth birthday, when she noted the white sails like stooping doves about

them. Now he was accompanied by Williams and Vivian as they
hoisted sail in the sultry early afternoon.

Many stories are told of what happened next. Certainly there was a
storm at about half past six. Possibly Taaffe's tale of an Italian
captain who offered to take the *Don Juan*'s crew aboard and advised
them to reef their sails, is true. According to him, both the offer and
the advice were rejected by Shelley. The *Don Juan* sank with all her
sails up, ten miles out from Viareggio.

For ten days there was no certain news of the three men. Then their
bodies were washed up, too much ravaged to be recognizable by
anything but their clothes and, in Shelley's case, a copy of Keats's
poems belonging to Hunt in his jacket pocket. The quarantine laws
against the plague meant that the bodies had to be dealt with
drastically, and Trelawny took charge, first burying them in quicklime
and then arranging for a furnace on the beach in which Shelley and
Williams were cremated. Leigh Hunt and Byron were present,
besides a few fishermen and the militia, and Trelawny collected the
ashes and Shelley's heart. His ashes were later entombed in the
Protestant cemetery in Rome, where his son William and Keats also
lay. His heart was given first to Hunt and then, after a quarrel, to
Mary. Long after her death, it was buried in Bournemouth beside his
son Percy.

The Protestant Cemetery in
Rome by Samuel Palmer.

> 'the spirit
> of the spot shall lead
> Thy footsteps to a slope of green
>   access
> Where, like an infant's smile,
>   over the dead
> A light of laughing flowers along
>   the grass is spread.'
>
> (*Adonais*)

Shelley's tomb, with the stone placed by Trelawny and inscription chosen by Leigh Hunt: *Cor cordium*

Mary Shelley's best qualities appeared in her scrupulous handling of Shelley's poems; he could not have wished for a more intelligent editor. Her diaries show that she struggled with continuous depression after his death; remorse for her own failings in her relations with him may have encouraged a tendency to idealize and even sentimentalize his memory. She became a pious, conscious widow; Timothy Shelley behaved ill to her, and for the most part she maintained herself and brought up Percy by her own efforts as a writer.

After an initial period of intense friendship she fell out with Jane Williams when she revealed Shelley's passion for her. Hogg, true to form, wooed Jane; they settled down together and had a daughter, Prudentia. Hogg's *Life* of Shelley was cut off half-way when Percy and his wife objected to its cynical tone. Peacock refused to write a *Life* but

left valuable reminiscences, as did Hunt and Medwin and the unreliable but enthusiastic Trelawny, who revered Shelley into his hale nineties, remaining an atheist and loathing the British Empire. In his last days he was visited in Sussex by Edward Carpenter, the sage and sexual reformer who influenced D. H. Lawrence and befriended E. M. Forster, offering a neat physical link between the radical ideas of one century and the next.

The *Liberal* failed after four issues. Byron departed to fight in Greece and died there in April 1824. Claire went first to Vienna and then to Russia as a governess; she ended her days in Florence, finally received into the Catholic Church and dying at the age of eighty-one, in 1879. The scramble to acquire her papers inspired Henry James to an elegantly gruesome story, *The Aspern Papers*. Jane also lived long, with her guitar and manuscripts, dying in 1884.

Shelley's son Charles was taken into Sir Timothy's care and sent to Syon Academy, but died of tuberculosis at the age of 11 and is buried in Warnham Church. Ianthe was brought up by Eliza Westbrook, as Harriet had wished, and married a Somerset banker. She had two sons, one living as a country gentleman until 1922 when he died in a hunting accident, aged seventy-seven; the other a country clergyman.

Hellen and Margaret Shelley and
(*opposite*) Mary Shelley in her
widowhood

Ianthe was on good terms with her Shelley aunts and, ultimately,
with her half-brother Percy. Sir Timothy died in 1844 at the age of
ninety-two. Percy married a widow whose devotion to Mary cheered
her last years – she died in 1851 – and encouraged her to build the
legend of Shelley as being closer to angel than man. Percy died
without issue after a blameless and utterly undistinguished existence.

From the beginning Shelley was championed by radicals; but the
odd thing about much Victorian appreciation of him is that it rested
on a rejection of his principles, disapproval of his life and admiration
for at best a few of his choruses and lyrics. Had George Henry Lewes's
projected *Life* appeared, a juster view might have been reached; it
would certainly have been frank and perceptive. Browning and Clough
both admired the poetry, although Browning felt obliged to see
Shelley as an incipient Christian; and Clough remarked wistfully that
'Shelley made wings for other people to fly on'. The *bien-pensants*
continued to fear the force of those wings; in the 1870s the Provost of
Eton refused a bust of its well-known ex-pupil and although by the

nineties he was prepared to take one, it was with the grudging aside that he wished he had been to Harrow instead (where Percy was sent). By then the radical chorus was growing louder, and Bernard Shaw was among the serious admirers. Had Shelley lived out the same life span as his father he would have seen two reform bills passed and many of his ideas championed. Yet any attempt to measure his powers by considering the reforms and revolutions that have taken place would be a futile exercise: on the one hand we still slaughter animals and support a royal family in England, on the other we have many health food shops and more sexual freedom. This is not the way poetry works on human consciousness; Shelley's achievement lies rather in giving us faith in the processes of poetry itself.

In this century Shelley's poetry has sometimes been subject to what one writer has called persecution rather than criticism: T. S. Eliot, F. R. Leavis and Allen Tate have all spoken disparagingly of his genius. His life, on the other hand, has attracted many biographers and much speculation, not always for the ignoble reason that most people prefer to study human problems rather than to battle with sometimes difficult poetry: there is a real sense in which the most powerful myth created by Shelley is the myth of himself.

It is not Prometheus or Asia, Mont Blanc or the skylark, Queen Mab, Demogorgon or Beatrice Cenci who seize and hold the imagination, but the image of Shelley's own struggles, his delight and hope and suffering and despair, from the line in his undergraduate volume, 'I met a maniac, like he was to me', to the painfully soaring spirit of the late lyrics. In the *Hymn to Intellectual Beauty*, in *Alastor*, in *Julian and Maddalo* and *Stanzas written in Dejection*; in Asia's questions to Demogorgon, in *The Two Spirits*, *Adonais* and *Epipsychidion*, it is the mythologizing of his own struggle to understand how the poet's dream of a good world relates to oppression, mutability, time and death that makes the greatness. No one who reads with attention and sympathy can doubt that greatness any more than the importance of the question or the beauty of the voice that puts it so insistently.

Shelley's best answer, his most lyrical and imaginative response to his finally unanswerable question, comes in that flawless lyric of 1820, *The Two Spirits: An Allegory*. It is a dialogue with himself in which his imagination provides the only good solution by referring back to idealizing love: the dream of *Alastor*, which led its hero to his death, reappears as the answer to disillusion, failure and death. It is not a bad answer, in Shelley's world or ours:

First Spirit

O thou, who plumed with strong desire
    Wouldst float above the earth, beware!
A Shadow tracks thy flight of fire –
    Night is coming!
Bright are the regions of the air,
And among the winds and beams
    It were delight to wander there –
    Night is coming!

Second Spirit

The deathless stars are bright above;
  If I would cross the shade of night,
Within my heart is the lamp of love,
      And that is day!
  And the moon will smile with gentle light
On my golden plumes where'er they move;
  The meteors will linger round my flight,
      And make night day.

First Spirit

But if the whirlwinds of darkness waken
  Hail, and lightning, and stormy rain;
See, the bounds of air are shaken –
      Night is coming!
  The red swift clouds of the hurricane
Yon declining sun have overtaken,
  The clash of the hail sweeps over the plain –
      Night is coming!

Second Spirit

I see the light, and I hear the sound;
  I'll sail on the flood of the tempest dark,
With the calm within and the light around
      Which makes night day:
  And thou, when the gloom is deep and stark,
Look from thy dull earth, slumber-bound,
  My moon-like flight thou then mayst mark
      On high, far away.

Some say there is a precipice
  Where one vast pine is frozen to ruin
O'er piles of snow and chasms of ice
      Mid Alpine mountains;
  And that the languid storm pursuing
That wingèd shape, for ever flies
  Round those hoar branches, aye renewing
      Its aëry fountains.

Some say when nights are dry and clear,
  And the death-dews sleep on the morass,
Sweet whispers are heard by the traveller,
      Which make night day:
  And a silver shape like his early love doth pass
Upborne by her wild and glittering hair,
  And when he awakes on the fragrant grass,
      He finds night day.

CHRONOLOGY

1792 Birth of Percy Bysshe Shelley, 4 August, at Field Place in Sussex.

1802 Goes to Syon House Academy.

1804–10 At Eton, latterly influenced by Dr Lind.

1810 Publishes *Zastrozzi* and *Original Poetry by Victor and Cazire*; goes up to Oxford, meets T. J. Hogg. Publishes *Posthumous Fragments of Margaret Nicholson* and *St Irvyne*. His cousin Harriet Grove breaks with him.

1811 Publishes *The Necessity of Atheism* and is sent down from Oxford. Quarrels with father; meets and elopes with Harriet Westbrook, marrying, 29 August, in Edinburgh. Moves to York and then Keswick. Meets Southey.

1812 Begins correspondence with Godwin. Travels to Dublin, publishes *Address to the Irish People* and *Proposals for an Association*, has *Declaration of Rights* printed. Returns to Wales and then to Lynmouth; writes *Letter to Lord Ellenborough*. Elizabeth Hitchener lives with Shelleys from July to November. Journeys to north Wales; to London, where friendship with Godwins is established; meets Peacock. Returns to Wales.

1813 Leaves Wales, going first to Ireland after incident at Tanyr-allt, then back to London. Writing *Queen Mab*, which is printed in May. Birth of daughter Ianthe, 23 June. In July to

Bracknell, Berkshire. Publishes *A Vindication of Natural Diet*. In autumn to Edinburgh with Harriet and Peacock. Boinville friendship.

1814 *Refutation of Deism* printed. 27 July, leaves England with Mary Godwin and Jane Clairmont; travels through Continent, returning to London in September. Birth of Charles Shelley to Harriet, 30 November.

1815 Death of grandfather Sir Bysshe Shelley. Birth and death of Mary's daughter. In August to Bishopsgate; the river trip.

1816 Birth of William Shelley, 24 January. Publication of *Alastor*. To Switzerland with Mary and Jane, now known as Claire. Through her establishes friendship with Lord Byron. *Hymn to Intellectual Beauty* and *Mont Blanc* written. Returns to England, September. Friendship with Leigh Hunt. Suicides of Fanny Imlay and Harriet Shelley. 30 December, marries Mary.

1817 12 January, birth of Claire's daughter by Byron, Allegra. Shelley fails to obtain custody of Ianthe and Charles. Meets Keats. Lives at Marlow for a year, beginning March. Publishes *A Proposal for Putting Reform to the Vote* and *Address . . . on the Death of Princess Charlotte;* also *History of a Six Weeks' Tour*, in collaboration with Mary. Writes *Laon and Cythna*, changed to *The Revolt of Islam*. Starts

Rosalind and Helen. Birth of Clara Shelley, 2 September. Poor health.

1818 11 March goes abroad with Mary, Claire and children. To Lyons and through Alps to Italy; Milan, Como, Pisa, Leghorn, Bagni di Lucca. Meets Gisbornes, Allegra sent to Byron in Venice. Shelley and Claire to Venice in August; Mary follows. Death of Clara Shelley. At Este writes *Julian and Maddalo, Euganean Hills*, Act I of *Prometheus*. To Ferrara, Rome, Naples. 27 December, birth of Elena Shelley.

1819 Leaves Naples end of February. Writes Acts II and III of *Prometheus* in Rome. Death of William Shelley, 7 June. To Leghorn. Writes *The Cenci* and *Masque of Anarchy*. In October to Florence. Birth of Percy Florence, 12 November. Writes *Peter Bell the Third, Ode to the West Wind, Philosophical View of Reform*, finishes *Prometheus Unbound*. Meets the Masons.

1820 To Pisa in January. Death of Elena Shelley in June. At Leghorn in summer, writes *Letter to Maria Gisborne. Ode to Liberty* and *Ode to Naples* greet revolutions in Spain and southern Italy. At Bagni di San Giuliano writes *Witch of Atlas* and *Swellfoot*. Returns to Pisa, October. Claire leaves for Florence, Medwin arrives. Meets Emilia Viviani.

1821 Writes *Epipsychidion*. Arrival of Edward and Jane Williams. Writes *Defence of Poetry*. Death of Keats. Writes *Adonais*. Visits Byron at Ravenna. Writes *Hellas* on Greek uprising. Pirated edition of *Queen Mab* in England. Byron arrives in Pisa.

1822 Trelawny arrives in Pisa. Death of Allegra, 20 April. Shelley and Williamses to Lerici. Claire joins them. Many poems addressed to Jane Williams and working on *Triumph of Life*. Mary has near-fatal miscarriage. 1 July, Shelley sails to Leghorn to meet Leigh Hunt; sees Byron and Masons. Drowned, 8 July.

1824 *Posthumous Poems of Percy Bysshe Shelley* issued by Mary Shelley.

1832 *The Masque of Anarchy* issued by Leigh Hunt.

1839 *The Poetical Works of P.B.S.* in 4 volumes issued by Mary.

SELECT BIBLIOGRAPHY

Complete Poetical Works, ed. Thomas Hutchinson (Oxford, 1904; rev. edn paperback 1970, hardback, 1971), corrected by G. M. Matthews. Mr Matthews is preparing a two-volume complete poems to be published by Longman's in the early 1980s, which will become the standard authoritative text.

Complete Poetical Works, ed. Neville Rogers (OUP; 4 vols, of which 2 already pubd).

Penguin publishes a useful selection of the poetry made by Kathleen Raine (Harmondsworth and New York, 1978; first pubd 1974).

The ten-volume *Complete Works*, ed. Roger Ingpen and Walter Peck (London, 1926–30; new edn London and New York, 1965), contains almost all Shelley's prose.

A new edition of the collected prose, by E. B. Murry and Timothy Webb, is due from OUP in 1982–3.

Shelley and his Circle (vols I–IV ed. K. N. Cameron, V–VI Donald Reiman, two more in preparation) (Cambridge, Mass., and Oxford, 1961–), large-scale catalogue, with editorial comment, of Shelley papers held in Carl Pforzheimer Library, New York.

Letters of P.B.S., ed. F. L. Jones, 2 vols (Oxford, 1964).

Letters of Mary Shelley, ed. F. L. Jones, 2 vols (Norman, Oklahoma, 1944).

Mary Shelley's Journal, ed. F. L. Jones (Norman, Oklahoma, 1947). A new edition by Paula Feldman and Diana Pugh (OUP, 1980) will be the first complete text drawn from the original.

Claire Clairmont's Journals, ed. Marion Kingston Stocking (Cambridge, Mass., 1968).

Medwin, Thomas. *Life of P.B.S.*, 2 vols (London, 1847). New edn with introduction and commentary by H. Buxton Forman (London, 1913).

Hunt, Leigh. *Autobiography*, 3 vols (London, 1850). New edn with introduction and notes by J. E. Morpurgo (London, 1949).

Trelawny, E. J. *Recollections of the Last Days of Shelley and Byron* (London and Boston, Mass., 1858). Rev. edn by J. E. Morpurgo (London, 1952).

Hogg, T. J. *Life of P.B.S.*, 2 vols only (London, 1858).

Peacock, T. L. *Memoirs of Shelley 1858–1862*. Rev. edn, including other essays and reviews, by H. Mills (London, 1970).

Dowden, Edward. *Life of P.B.S.*, 2 vols (London, 1886).

Keats–Shelley Memorial Bulletins, a continuing series from 1910.

Brailsford, H. N. *Shelley, Godwin, and their Circle* (London and New York, 1913).

Leavis, F. R. 'Shelley' in *Scrutiny*, vol. IV, p. 158, or *Revaluation; Tradition and Development in English Poetry* (London, 1936).

White, Newman Ivey. *Shelley*, 2 vols (New York, 1940; London, 1947).

Cameron, K. N. *The Young Shelley: Genesis of a Radical* (New York, 1950; London, 1951).

Bloom, Harold. *Shelley's Mythmaking* (New Haven, Conn., 1959).

Chernaik, Judith. *The Lyrics of Shelley* (London and Cleveland, Ohio, 1972).

Cameron, K. N. *Shelley: The Golden Years* (Cambridge, Mass., 1974).

Holmes, Richard. *Shelley: The Pursuit* (London, 1974; New York, 1975).

Webb, Timothy. *The Violet in the Crucible* (Oxford, 1976).

Dawson, Paul. *The Unacknowledged Legislator: Shelley and Politics* (due from OUP, 1980).

AUTHOR'S ACKNOWLEDGMENTS

Shelley scholars are good-hearted people: G. M. Matthews and Paul Foot offered advice and encouragement, and Dr Paul Dawson gave me particularly generous assistance, for which I am very grateful. The staffs of the Bodleian, the British Museum and the London Library were, as always, kind and helpful, as were those with whom I worked at Thames and Hudson. I wish also to thank my daughter Susanna Tomalin whose suggestions for clarifying and improving the text were invaluable and who made the index.

NOTES ON THE TEXT

The anecdote of Fanny Burney and Edmund Burke on p. 6 comes from her diary for June 1792, and appears in Joyce Hemlow's edition of the *Journals and Letters,* vol. I (Oxford, 1792).

The quotation from Harriet Grove's diary on p. 15 is taken from *Shelley and his Circle* edited by K. N. Cameron, vol. II (Oxford and the Carl Pforzheimer Library, 1961).

The quotation on p. 42 is from the notes to *Queen Mab.*

G. M. Matthews has established that the verses on p. 60 are addressed to Fanny Imlay, not William Shelley, in an essay entitled 'Whose Little Footsteps?' in *The Evidence of the Imagination*, ed. Donald Reiman, M. C. Jaye and B. Bennett (New York, 1978).

Teresa Guiccioli's remarks on Shelley on p. 103 are taken from Doris Langley Moore's *Lord Byron Accounts Rendered*, published by John Murray (London, 1974).

PHOTOGRAPHIC ACKNOWLEDGMENTS

Reproduced by Gracious Permission of Her Majesty Queen Elizabeth II 51; Collection of Lord Abinger 93; Alinari 87; Birmingham Museum and Art Gallery 72–3; Bournemouth, Casa Magni Shelley Museum 91, 117; Collection of G. Chastel de Boinville 41; Collection of Viscount De L'Isle 8 *bottom; Examiner* (1819) 69, 89; *Harper's Magazine* (1893–4) 101; *Illustrated London News* (1892) 111; London, British Museum, Department of Prints and Drawings 59, 97, 113, Courtauld Institute of Art 23, Keats House, Hampstead 115, Keats–Shelley Memorial Association 9 *top r.*, 63 *top*, 63 *bottom*, National Portrait Gallery 2, 12, 18, 25, 31, 34, 65, 119, Tate Gallery 24, Victoria and Albert Museum, Department of Prints and Drawings 44 *top*, 44 *bottom*, 45, 116; Madrid, Museo del Prado 39; Collection of Lady Mander 88, 106 *bottom;* MAS 39; Collection of Mr and Mrs Paul Mellon 81; Collection of John Murray, 71; New York, Carl H. Pforzheimer Library 9 *l.*, 57, 82, 86; Pierpont Morgan Library 104, His Grace the Duke of Norfolk 23, Nottingham Museums, Newstead Abbey 54, 55; Collection of Major R. P. Owen 14; Oxford, Bodleian Library 5, 9 *bottom r.*, 20 *l.*, 20 *r.*, 35, 62, 67 *top*, 67 *bottom*, 98, 108, 109, 118; Paris, Musée Carnavalet 6; Private Collection 1; Rome, Galleria Nazionale 87, Keats–Shelley Memorial House 41, 95, 106 *top;* Collection of Rev Dr W. S. Scott 17; Edwin Smith 13

Illustrations have been reproduced from the following publications: R. Ackermann, *Microcosm of London* (1808–9) 30, 64; R. Ackermann, *Repository of the Arts* (1809–15) 15; R. Ayton, *A Voyage Round Great Britain* (1814–25) 29; S. F. Brocas, *Coloured Views of Dublin* (1820) 26; W. B. and G. Cooke, *Descriptions of Views on the Thames* (1822) 50 *top*, 50 *bottom*; E. Dowden, *The Life of Percy Bysshe Shelley* (1880) 7; H. B. Forman, *The Works of Percy Bysshe Shelley* (1880) 66; L. Galvani, *Aloysii Galvani de viribus electricitatis in motu musculari commentarius* (1792) 10; T. Hurst, *Eccentric Biography* (1803) 33 *top*; R. E. Prothero, *The Works of Lord Byron* (1898–1901) 107; J. Skelton, *Oxonia Antiqua* (1823) 16

INDEX

Figures in italic refer to illustrations

Hazlitt, William 64
Healy (or Hill), Dan 27, 31, 34, 35
High Elms 38
Hitchener, Elizabeth 21, 23, 27, 28, 34
Hogg, Thomas Jefferson 16–20, *17*, 22, 23, 29, 34, 49, 83, 92, 116
Hookham, Thomas 30, 34, 46, 61
Hooper, Mrs 31
Hoppner, Mr and Mrs 77, 102
Hume, David 25
Hume, Dr Thomas 62
Hunt, Leigh 18, *18*, 22, 31, 34, 60, 64, 74, 90,' 107, 114, 115, 117

I Capuccini 78
Imlay, Fanny 33, 42, 59, 60
India 12, 108

Kean, Edmund 48
Keate, Dr 11
Keats, John 64, *65*, 92, 98, 101
Kensington Gardens 49
Kentish Town 48
Keswick 23, 53
Killarney 35

Lac Léman 54, 56, *56*
Lake Lucerne 46
La Spezia 110
Lausanne 56
Lawrence, James 6, 27, 49
Leavis, F. R. 120
Lechlade *50*, 51
Leghorn (Livorno) 76, 86, 87, 94, 102, 114
Lerici *1*, 108
Lewes, G. H. 118
Lewis, M. G. ('Monk') 13, 59
Lewis's Hotel, London 32
Liberal 107, 117
Lincoln's Inn Fields 15, *15*
Lind, Dr James 12
Liverpool, Lord 92
Lucca 92, 95
Lucretius 12
Lunar Society 12
Lynmouth 29, *29*, 49

Madocks, William, MP 32
Madrid 31

Maison Chappuis 55
Marlow (Great) *50*, 65, 66, 68
Masi, Sergeant-Major 110
'Mr Mason' (George Tighe) 92, 107
'Mrs Mason' (Lady Mountcashel) 92, 96, 114
Mavrocordato, Prince Alexander 97, 101, *101*, 105
Medwin, Kate 5
Medwin, Tom 10, 92, 96, 117
Meillerie 56
Merioneth 32
Michelangelo, Buonarroti 83
Milan 74, *75*
Milton, John 13
Modern Philosophers, The (by Elizabeth Hamilton) 14
Montaigne 60
Montalègre 55
Mont Blanc 58
Mont Cenis *72–3*, 74
Monte San Pellegrino 95
Moscow 31
Mozart, Wolfgang Amadeus 64

Naples 81
Napoleon 31, 46, 74
Neuchâtel 46
Newton, John 34, *110*
Nicholls, Mrs Eleanor 8
Nicholson, Margaret 17
Nightmare Abbey 76
Norfolk, Charles Howard, Duke of 7, *23*, 25
Nouvelle Heloïse, La 56
Novello, Vincent 66

O'Connell, Daniel 26
Ollier, Charles 68, 80, 91, 92, 100, 105, 107
Opie, Amelia 22
Owen, Robert 60
Oxford 15, *16*, 51

Pacchiani, Francesco 97, 105
Padua 77
Paine, Tom 5, 21, 30, *31*, 68, 71
Palazzo Galetti 97
Paley, Archbishop 19
Paris *44*, 46
Peacock, Thomas Love 11, 17, 34, *34*, 38, 43, 48, 60, 65, 68, 69, 76,

80, 83, 92, 100, 102, 104, 108, 116
Peterloo 88, *89*
Pilfold, Captain (uncle) 20, 70
Pisa 76, *91*, 92, 97, 101, 106, *106*, *107*, 110, 114, 115
Pliny 12
Polidori, John 54
Political Justice, Enquiry Concerning 6, 12
Pompeii 81
Pontarlier 46
Priestley, Joseph 10
Prince Regent (see also George IV) 21, 34
Pugnano 101

Ravenna 102, 105
Reni, Guido 86
Reveley, Henry 76
Reynolds, J. H. 90
Rhine, River 47
Roberts, Captain Daniel 112, 114
Rome 80, 83, *84*, *85*, 86, 115
Rotterdam 47
Rousseau, Jean-Jacques 56
Ryan, Major 43

St Bartholomew's Hospital 18
St George's, Hanover Square 40
St Mildred's, Bread St 62
St Pancras Church 42, *43*
St Paul's Cathedral 48
San Terenzo 111
Sécheron 54
Serchio, River 95
Severn Canal 51
Seward, Anna 6
Shaw, George Bernard 120
Shelley, Sir Bysshe (grandfather) 8, *8*, 19, 49
Shelley, Elizabeth (mother, *née* Pilfold) 7, 17, 19, 20, *20*, 40
Shelley, Elizabeth (sister) 8, 9, *9*, 17, 20
Shelley, Hellen (sister) 8, 18, 25, 118, *118*
Shelley, John (brother) 11
Shelley, Mary (sister) 18, 118, *118*
Shelley, Mary (wife, *née* Godwin) 33, 42 and thereafter *passim*, 62, *119*
Shelley, Percy Bysshe *2*, 9, *14*, *104*, *110*; birth 5; family